Science Teaching as a Profession

Why it isn't. How it could be.

By Sheila Tobias
and Anne Baffert

National Science Teachers Association
Arlington, VA

National Science Teachers Association

Claire Reinburg, Director
Jennifer Horak, Managing Editor
Andrew Cocke, Senior Editor
Judy Cusick, Senior Editor
Wendy Rubin, Associate Editor
Amy America, Book Acquisitions Coordinator

ART AND DESIGN
Will Thomas Jr., Director, cover and interior design

PRINTING AND PRODUCTION
Catherine Lorrain, Director

National Science Teachers Association
Francis Q. Eberle, PhD, Executive Director
David Beacom, Publisher

LIBRARY OF CONGRESS CATALOGING-IN-PUBLICATION DATA
Tobias, Sheila.
  Science teaching as a profession: why it isn't, how it could be / by Sheila Tobias and Anne Baffert.
    p. cm.
  Includes index.
  ISBN 978-1-936137-06-0
  1. Science teachers—Vocational guidance—United States. 2. High school teachers—Vocational guidance—United States.
3. Science teachers—Training of—United States. 4. High school teachers—Training of—United States. 5. Science—Study
and teaching (Secondary)—United States. 6. Leadership. I. Baffert, Anne. II. Title.
  Q149.U5T63 2010
  507.1—dc22
                    2010002968

eISBN 978-1-936137-76-3

The reporting and research for this book was financed by Research Corporation for Science Advancement (RCSA), America's second-oldest foundation, begun in 1912, and the first dedicated wholly to science. RCSA supports early career scientist-scholars engaged in boundary-crossing, high-risk, high-reward research integrating educational initiatives at America's colleges and universities.

Science Teaching as a Profession

Why it isn't. How it could be.

Table of Contents

Foreword

I've always wondered why science education reform efforts didn't stick. Here we are a half-century after Sputnik, decades after thoughtful reports on our challenges and attempts to address them, and yet our students' achievement in science is still substandard. The words of the Glenn Commission Report of 2000, nearly a decade ago, still are relevant: "The state of science and mathematics education in this country is, in a word, unacceptable."

I was a product of the Sputnik times, a junior in high school. Casual family dinnertime conversations shifted to our country's needs and, in my case, career options. After graduating from high school, I headed off to prepare to be a high-school physics teacher. Four years later I had my first teaching appointment. During these first few years, the government was investing heavily in new curricula and, most important to me, in summer enrichment programs for science teachers. My summers were spent looking over new materials, debating with other colleagues about the materials, and preparing for a much better year ahead.

Why didn't that effort stick? Among many reasons, lack of professional support of science teachers and the erosion of the public perception of science teaching as a profession are paramount. Tobias and Baffert argue that this erosion has brought us to our present-day situation of high-stakes testing of factoids, dismal results, and the subsequent blaming of teachers for those results.

Tobias and Baffert address the central issue in science education today. The professional stature of the science teacher—conspicuously absent from current prescriptions for improving science education—is their primary focus. Beginning in 1983 with "A Nation at Risk," numerous reports and studies have collectively covered the waterfront of possible reasons for the failure of science education and efforts to reform it, while neglecting the importance of the professional stature of science teachers. Consequently stakeholders from policy makers to parents have overlooked the profound consequences of the steady decline in the status of science teachers.

While most politicians, parents, and the general public seem to rally around the concept of professionalism, even this general agreement begs the question, "What is it?" How does a group lose it and, most important, regain it? Through a number of conduits, the authors of this book succeed at defining professionalism in the context of science teachers. The major accomplishment of this book is its broad exploration of professionalism in science education.

Foreword

As one example, the authors adroitly point out that professionalism encompasses accountability and responsibility. The authors, and the teachers they talked to, acknowledge that accountability is a reasonable expectation of professional teachers. And they acknowledge their responsibility to seek alternatives to high-stakes, end-of-the-year tests of student improvement. While the No Child Left Behind Act fuels the tendency to hold science teachers accountable for underachieving students, science teachers have been largely absent from the development of tests that measure that achievement. Science teachers must be responsible, at least in part, for turning education away from blindly valuing what it measures and toward measuring what we truly value.

Those values have been clearly articulated by thousands of scientists, science teachers, and university educators in the National Science Education Standards (NSES). But when NSES was released in January 1996, the states selectively chose which sections to use and which to ignore. In addition to the one chapter on content and skills, NSES included four chapters addressing standards in science teaching, professional development for teachers of science, program standards, system standards and assessment standards—all issues that needed to be addressed if science education reform were to succeed. Unfortunately, these recommendations went largely unnoticed, and many states created a process that effectively removed the science teachers from the conversations about assessment and accountability.

This book is a must-read for anybody seriously interested in supporting a reform movement that will stick. It's well written and accessible for both lay and professional audiences. It is a first step in addressing a facet of science education too long ignored. The transformation of science education that we need to produce the next generation of informed citizens will come through the leadership, responsibility and accountability of professional science teachers.

Gerald F. Wheeler
Executive Director Emeritus, National Science Teachers Association

A Note on Methodology

Science Teaching as a Profession draws from two admittedly biased samples of secondary science teachers. Every effort has been made to seek balance, but in no way should our respondents be considered a representative sample. They are, rather, informants.

The first sample consists of respondents to a series of questions-of-the-month and discussion topics and polls posted on the project website: *www.science-teaching-as-a-profession.com*. Officially launched in September 2007, the website was intended to be an extension of our project, a means of generating data and interest in the upcoming book. In a short time, the website became its own entity, providing science teachers with a much-appreciated forum to discuss the "hot" issues science teachers face today.

Respondents were generated by invitations to particular Listservs, the authors' personal mailing lists, and references by teachers who were enjoying the website and told their colleagues about it. Statistically speaking, the respondents represent a skewed population. They are largely members of the National Science Teachers Association or subscribers to the Advanced Placement Biology, Chemistry, and Physics Listservs. These are the cyberspace hangouts for professional science teachers always looking for ways to hone their craft and to interact with other professionals. So, it is in these waters that we cast our provocative (oftentimes controversial) discussion topics.

Teachers from all 50 states as well as some teachers abroad have sounded off on the discussion topics listed in the table below. The website is building a loyal audience, with some teachers joining in each time a new discussion topic is posted.

Our second sample consists of individual and group interviews with current or former secondary science teachers, administrators, state legislators, and program and policy experts. For the interviews, we employed a protocol based on the chapters in the book intended to probe their experience, insights, and suggestions for change (see Interview Protocols, p. 143).

We recognize that the people who chose to talk to us had strong points of view. Without doing injustice to what they said, there was no way we could impose "balance." Nor could we substantiate their claims. What the reader will find here, which we consider to be invaluable, are teachers' *perceptions*, and it is their perceptions that drive their behavior—the quality of their teaching as well as their longevity in the job.

Discussion Topics and Dates

December 2007	Advancement
January 2008	How has NCLB affected your teaching, work life, and professional status?
February 2008	Can Professional Learning Communities (PLC) help to professionalize the science teaching profession? If you have participated in a PLC, did it enhance your status, increase your autonomy, or give you higher-level access to the decision makers in your school or district?
February 2008	I am considering applying for National Board Certification, but before I do so, I wanted to get some feedback about: The process (How time-consuming is it? Is the process a waste of time, or does it help you develop as a professional?) The benefits (Is it worth the time invested? Are you respected more now that you have the certification?)
March 2008	With your educational background, you are most likely eligible for any number of jobs with more lucrative salary packages and significantly less demand on your time. What keeps you from leaving your science teaching profession?
April 2008	Do you teach (or have you taught) science in a private or charter school?
May 2008	Who controls what you teach? Who controls your curriculum?
May 2008	Should a high-school physics, biology, or chemistry teacher receive the same salary as a kindergarten teacher? What do you think of the traditional salary schedule? What changes could be made in teacher compensation to attract and, perhaps more importantly, retain high-school science teachers? How do you as a science teacher feel about the fact that your salary is equivalent to that of someone teaching a nonscience subject in a lower grade?
June 2008	Is tenure important to you? Would you trade your tenure for a $5,000 pay increase?
June 2008	Do science teachers work only nine months out of the year? What do you do during your summer break?
July 2008	In your school or district are there pay differentials (including signing bonuses) or incentives (like discounted housing) provided for secondary science or math teachers?
July 2008	Teaching in another district or another state often means losing health and retirement benefits as well as accrued experience. Has the lack of reciprocity between states and/or districts affected you? How? Would you favor legislation that would facilitate a teacher's mobility across districts and states?
September 2008	How have the storms around the topic of the teaching of evolution impacted your capability and your autonomy in the classroom? In your answer, please indicate whether your state or school district mandates the teaching of evolution (as recently occurred in Florida) or tells you to teach both evolution and intelligent design.
October 2008	What would be the benefit to science teachers and their students if more principals and superintendents were science teachers? Do you think a science-trained superintendent or principal would make a difference in the policies, funding, and decisions that affect you as a professional? If your superintendent or principal is a science teacher, do you see any benefits to you as a teacher or to your students?
October 2008	Do you teach secondary science outside the United States? Do you know anyone teaching science in another country?
November 2008	What is the highest-ranking position a science teacher holds in your school? Are you interested in ever (maybe not now) becoming a school or district administrator? If not, why not?
December 2008	Do you know a science teacher who wishes to be a district superintendent?

Teacher Interviews and Website Responses

Website responses, together with snippets from teacher interviews, were sorted by topic and are integrated into the argument and analysis of each chapter.

We have long since exceeded our initial goal, which was to capture 100 teachers' voices. We think the reason is teachers need to interact across cyberspace to counter their isolation in the classroom. We are grateful to all our teachers—who remain anonymous in this volume—for making this work possible.

Also, we are grateful to the hundreds of teachers who allowed our team to interview them (and to whom we refer using pseudonyms in this book); also to the more than 1,000 respondents to our website questions and frequent polls. Details as to how these were culled and assessed are available on request from the authors.

Resources Consulted

Once upon a time, to write a book on a subject like this one, we would have scoured the library—particularly a world-class library as we have at the University of Arizona—to find the precise Dewey Decimal code for *teaching as a profession*. But a "hot topic" in today's United States can't be contained within books, either scholarly or popular, that are published even within the past few years. Our major sources of information were up-to-date articles at the intersection of "science teaching" and "teaching" in general, which came to us, or which we found by ourselves on the websites that cater to both communities, as well as the comments that made their way to our website, *www.science-teaching-as-a-profession. com*. However, there are authors, books, and articles, which, even when some of them were dated, provided special guidance and insight. These references are found within the chapters and in Recommended Resources on p. 139.

Acknowledgments

We would like to acknowledge contributions and editorial assistance from the following who also served as remote interviewers: Jacqueline Raphael, an education researcher (Portland, Oregon); Suzanne S. Taylor, PhD, a labor and education consultant (Old Saybrook, Connecticut); Deborah Fort, a writer (Washington, D.C.) and Erin Dokter, PhD, a science educator. We also benefited from substantive reviews by Janice Koch, PhD, an author and science teacher educator and consultant (Long Island, New York), and Kirran Moss, EdD, CSU Long Beach, California. We are grateful to all for their input and suggestions.

The authors also wish to thank Martha Retallick of Western Sky Communications for her creative design of our interactive website.

Chapter 1

An Overview

Belatedly, it will seem to many teachers, efforts to improve K–12 education have put the classroom teacher back on center stage. After decades of innovation in the use of computers, the web, and other pedagogically rich devices, researchers on all sides of the political spectrum are converging on what is really an old-fashioned view: Student achievement depends mainly on the quality of instruction as created and conveyed by the teacher in the classroom.[1]

That's the good news for teachers.

But instead of gaining more autonomy and control over what he or she teaches and how, today's classroom teacher is becoming a prisoner of high-stakes testing of pupils' achievement gains. That's the gist of the revolution launched in 2002 by the No Child Left Behind Act (NCLB). Teacher "quality" is deemed directly responsible for pupils' achievement. And the obverse: Where pupils' gains are subpar, it is the teachers' fault.

In our wide-ranging inquiry into the state of secondary science teaching as a profession, we found job satisfaction diminishing with the loss of autonomy and control. The science teachers we interviewed and heard from on our interactive website fear that measuring teacher performance by student

---

1. In a pre-presidential election debate on the subject, education consultants Lisa Graham Keegan and Linda Darling-Hammond, working for candidates John McCain and Barack Obama, respectively, agreed on the central argument that "teacher effectiveness" is measured by students' academic progress in that teacher's class. See web seminar, Teachers College, October 20, 2008. *www.edweek.org/ew/section/video-galleries/tc_debate.html*

achievement gains alone could be another step in degrading the teaching profession altogether.

Central to any profession are "barriers to entry," the unique pre-entry training and certification requirements that differentiate the professional specialist from others. Since the late 19th century, those entering the teaching profession (or if not at entry, then very soon thereafter) were required to obtain state certification, which usually involves both a state-approved university-level education major or minor. Currently the state-certification model is witnessing some serious challenges.

In one such proposal to improve student achievement, Robert Gordon, Thomas Kane, and Douglas Staiger would eliminate both specific university training and state certification in favor of a teacher meeting performance criteria on the job:

> Under their proposal, a new teacher would continue to be required to have a four-year undergraduate bachelor's degree and to demonstrate content knowledge. They would allow teachers who met these basic requirements to be deemed "highly qualified" if they also demonstrate effectiveness in the classroom regardless of whether they had met a state's other certification requirements (2006).

Indeed, qualification to teach would cease to be formal and become operational. The authors go on to describe how "selective retention" would take place:

> Any new teacher scoring above the 50th percentile on the scale of "teacher effectiveness" at the end of two years would be deemed "highly qualified" regardless of their certification status or compliance with other state systems (Gordon, Kane, and Staiger 2006).

What should we make of such proposals? How serious a threat is "selective retention" to teaching as a profession? And where does secondary science teaching fit into the mix? On the one hand, it has been the nation's math-science "scorecard" in comparison with other countries that has fueled this decade's concern with educational reform. On the other, science teachers themselves have found fault with some of their training in pedagogy (preservice) and most especially with standard professional development (inservice).

Science teaching as a profession was already under siege when this new century began. Mostly absent from school and school district leadership, secondary science teachers (and in particular science chairs) have looked on helplessly as the ground shifts beneath them. Spokesmen (and women) for science education have been largely scientists. This is not entirely inappropriate. After all, science as a profession depends on high-quality recruits. Nor can we do without the science education research community. But science teachers have a unique expertise, and they are not usually invited to the table where decisions that affect their work are made.

Science teachers are not averse to having their own students' achievements factored into the equation. To the contrary, they look forward to having science put back on the front burner from which has been dislodged by math and reading.

Our proposition is simple but revolutionary. Until and unless science teachers are given back substantial control of the subjects they teach, including curriculum content, pedagogy, pacing, and assessment, and successfully recruited into leadership at the school, the district, the state, and the national levels, we won't have robust student achievement.

Recruitment vs. Retention

The need for secondary science teachers, the context of this book, calls urgently for new thinking both about the problem and the solutions. That our nation has to attract more college graduates to secondary science teaching is indisputable:

- Science and mathematics graduation requirements are slated to increase (in response to America's competitiveness agenda), which means schools and school districts will need even more secondary science/math teachers than ever before; and

- Although it is not clear whether science and math teachers leave their jobs at a greater rate than other teachers, the pipeline of qualified math and science teachers entering the field is insufficient to cover the number of teachers leaving the profession (Ingersoll 2000).

So there will be a shortfall. That cannot be denied. But the standard response to that anticipated math/science teacher shortage has been to focus on new recruits. And that may not suffice. Consider this: A much talked-about new national study calls for the recruitment of 10,000 new secondary science/math teachers per year to meet the shortage, starting right now (Committee on Prospering in the Global Economy of the 21st Century 2007). As we see it, this means that the "scramble" for warm bodies just moves up the food chain, from science chairs and school administrators searching for certified teachers for their schools to universities and state colleges of education trying to persuade high-performing science and math undergraduates to select teaching as a career.[2]

---

2. Recruitment efforts include U-Teach, Exxon-Mobil project, APLE (repay loans).

But is recruitment the only, or the preferred, strategy for meeting the shortfall? What about teacher retention? What would it take to keep the nation's trained and working 187,711 secondary (middle- and high-school) science teachers (5.8% of the total teachers employed in the United States; Rowland 2007) from thinking about leaving their jobs? We decided to ask them. This book grows out of a Listening Project that began in the fall of 2006 and continued through the winter of 2009.

Stage One involved listening to science chairs from 10 Tucson, Arizona, high schools. We asked them to respond to one of the basic premises of the national study, *Rising Above the Gathering Storm* (Committee on Prospering in the Global Economy of the 21st Century 2007) namely, that many (perhaps even most) secondary science teachers teach outside their major. Since our science chairs as a group hire, fire, and supervise 10 teachers each, we figured they would be able to quickly determine how well-trained their teachers are. We made that their first assignment. Of the 100 secondary science teachers in their sample, with one exception, they had either minored in the field they were teaching or had done significant postcollege work to qualify. The one exception was the Arizona state teacher-of-the-year, a biology teacher with a first degree in physical education.

Their second assignment was to prepare, on the basis of interviews with their teachers, a five-minute presentation that would convey to our governor how she could help them do a better job.

The upshot of the second assignment and subsequent conversations with our science chairs was this: Science teaching is rapidly losing its professional status and with it its professional appeal.

In the classroom, our science chairs assured us, their teachers feel like the professionals they consider themselves to be. They are responsible for almost everything that happens and they are in control. But outside the classroom, as a result of state and districtwide reporting requirements—most especially in dealing with fallout from No Child Left Behind—they feel like employees, with little autonomy or control.

Introducing the Science Teacher

To the casual observer, teaching is not so demanding a profession. Many people believe they could be teachers with little to no training.

To an outsider, a high-school teacher's work day starts at 8 a.m. and ends with the final bell at 3 p.m. And, let's not forget the breaks at Christmas and spring and, of course, that long summer vacation.

A closer look provides a much different picture. Teachers, particularly science teachers, must arrive at school before the students and stay hours later to set up and take down labs, restock and order lab equipment, grade papers, plan lessons and participate in school-related (and required) activities. Many science teachers are unable to take care of all their responsibilities during their workweek and return to school over the weekend. Teachers we interviewed and heard from on our interactive website pointed out that quite often the last cars to leave the parking lot belong to science teachers.

What few people outside of the teaching profession realize is that a teacher's hours are very different from, say, an architect's. Simply stated, there is zero downtime. When that classroom door opens, in flood dozens of teenagers with dozens of problems that need solutions. It is estimated that an average high-school teacher makes more than 1,500 decisions each day. Some compare their work to managing triage in a hospital, absent a support team.

Teachers who have left teaching for another profession are amazed by workplace luxuries at their new jobs: being able to check email, return phone calls, or use the bathroom at will throughout the day. Back in their teaching days, these ordinary tasks normally would have to be put off until lunch (unless the teacher had lunch duty) or until the end of the school day.

The pace and stress that teachers work under is much more like that of air-traffic controllers or emergency room personnel they tell us who are given multiple days off between shifts.

Based on what we heard, we decided to take our Listening Project to the web (*www.science-teaching-as-a-profession.com*) and to teachers in their schools via remote interviewers located around the country.[3]

The Power Matrix

We narrowed our original question—how to stem science teacher attrition—to this one: What would it take to return science teaching to the elite, highly respected professional status it once enjoyed (and still does in many other countries)?

We started with a tentative list: working conditions, pay, public support, competition for entry and promotion. But listening to teachers we were soon

---

3. We are, of course, not the only ones beginning to focus on working conditions rather than pay. See Viadero 2008.

struck by how much their lack of power over curriculum, teaching methods and students' evaluation had eroded their status and their satisfaction. And so we added a power matrix (see page 21) to our inquiries, asking them who (principal, district superintendent, school board, state school officers) makes decisions that affect their teaching. What we learned is that secondary science teachers have little or no say over their own teaching assignments, over budgeting for their lab materials, or—when and if science is added to No Child Left Behind—over the content and pacing of their lesson plans.

So who makes the decisions that affect what goes on in the science classroom? As teachers filled out our online power matrix, a picture emerged of outside ownership. In the near outside is the principal. More distant is the superintendent's office and more distant still the school board and the state's chief school officer.

Which means, and this is the recurrent theme of this book, if secondary science teachers are to win back lost professional status and satisfaction, they must take back control over their workday, their working conditions and their overall status.

We conclude our book with an assertion that the nation's failure to solve the problem of math/science education despite 35 years of effort may rest on policy makers' reluctance to mine the collective experience and insights of an army of experts who are highly educated in science, highly experienced in the classroom, and better than average problem solvers. We don't have to look far for these "educational experts." They are the nation's secondary science teachers. But they are rarely present when and where science education policies are deliberated. In Chapter 9 we outline strategies for teacher empowerment persuading (even obligating) secondary science teachers to participate in all levels of school and district governance by making careers that lead to power and influence more appealing to them:

- empowering science chairs and science supervisors by means of new science teacher councils to take a rightful place at the policy makers' table

- engaging the nation's scientists and science and engineering professionals in ongoing collaborations with science teachers

Their (The Experts') Findings and What Ours Added

With all the attention given to the STEM[4] teacher shortfall and the vast number of teacher surveys and other kinds of studies of the problem, we

---

4. STEM is the way the government refers to science, technology, engineering, and math education, in one acronym.

were surprised by how little of the existing teacher-attrition data is disaggregated by subject area, even by grade level. (We try to figure out who's leaving science teaching and why in Chapter 2.) We were also surprised by how few researchers go beyond "pay" and bare bones "working conditions" (usually limited to items such as school safety and cleanliness of the school) to concerns about autonomy and control raised by the teachers we consulted.

The most extensive recent review of the empirical literature on teacher recruitment and retention is on the American Educational Research Association website (*www.aera.net;* Guarino, Santibanez, and Daley 2006). It is this review and studies like it that we find woefully lacking in data disaggregated by field and/or teachers' grade level. The National Science Foundation's *Science and Engineering Indicators* (2008) does not do much better. In a section on "teacher salaries, working conditions, and job satisfaction," their conclusion, presumably quoting researchers who have studied science and math teachers, is less than illuminating:

> The research evidence suggests that adequate compensation and safe and supportive school environments serve to attract and retain teachers, whereas low pay and poor working conditions undermine teachers' long-term commitment to their jobs [5]

We prefer a more nuanced analysis (see Chapter 2).

There are of course the essentials: pay, tenure, and the positive and sometimes negative effects of unions on the profession (Chapter 5). Teachers bring these up all the time in interviews or in their web postings.

But there are also what we call crosscutting issues such as off-the-job (National Board) certification, and on-the-job professional development, and the biggest intruder of all, No Child Left Behind (NCLB, Chapter 4). These are among the attempts at education reform, not specific to science teaching, but inevitably bearing on science teachers' range of freedom inside and outside their classroom.

The relationship between National Board Certification for teachers and the NCLB regime provides an interesting case in point. When it began in 1986, National Board Certification was originally intended to enable teachers to raise their competencies and eventually their status and pay by signing on to a rigorous (and costly) two-year set of advanced training modules.

---

5. The researchers whose work is referred to include: Boyd et al. 2005; Dolton and Wilbert 1999; Hanushek, Kain, and Rivkin 2004; Ingersoll 2006; Loeb, Darling-Hammond, and Luczak 2005; and Perie and Baker 1997.

But that was before the high-stakes student testing required by NCLB redefined teacher competence. Once NCLB was in place, no longer was teacher competence to be measured in courses taken, experience garnered, lessons learned or formal self-improvement. All of this is being replaced by pupils' performance on standardized tests. Not surprisingly, board certification is currently losing much of its appeal, most particularly in the science community. National Board Certification was not even recommended by a recent National Science Board Study (2007).

More pernicious and only rarely dealt with in other studies is the slow, steady erosion of teachers' professional standing in all the places where it matters: the public at large, building administrators, district superintendents, and state school officers. Even parents are no longer in awe. In Chapter 3 we make an effort to trace the history of that erosion, starting with the way schooling and school teaching began in the United States; how long it took to become "regularized" in training academies and eventually universities; the tension, somewhat fostered by unionization between teacher-as-employee and teacher-as-professional; and, finally, the role of one group of scholars in downgrading teaching, nursing, and social work to the realm of "semiprofessions" (Etzioni 1969).

The Essential Elements of a Profession

There is no question in our minds and in the minds of the teachers contacted over the past two years that teaching is a profession or that it could be one if reforms are implemented. What is our evidence? Teaching involves mastery over complex bodies of knowledge, licensure by a legitimate authority, renewal through continuing education, and responsibility for young, vulnerable minds. Moreover, like doctors and lawyers, teachers are visibly responsible to a wider public, morally committed to public service, and capable of setting and policing standards for practice.

If these are among the essential elements of a profession, which of these are teachers missing? And how can science teachers (in particular) get back the elements of professional work and professional privilege they have lost?

Speaking with science teachers in groups and on our website about the essential elements of professions they hold in high esteem, we developed a list of 12 elements (See pp. 41–43), of which relative independence and autonomy is one; higher-than-average standard of living another; and input into federal, state, and local educational policy a third. These may not be as "basic" as pay and tenure, but they sure matter to teachers!

Ninth on our list (but by no means on theirs) is time: time out of the classroom; time for collaboration, even across schools and school districts; time for research; time for professional development. We spotlight Finland (in Chapter 8) because it is a country that has turned attrition around by investing in teachers' professional privileges. The teacher-as-researcher movement, which began in Great Britain in the 1990s, reached fruition in Finland, where teaching jobs are so competitive today that there are sometimes 10 applicants for every opening.

Because we couldn't visit a significant number of the nation's high school science departments, we chose to focus our attention on a few case studies representing the "best" and the "worst" in terms of our theme: science teacher retention. These are presented as anonymous "Close-Ups" (p. 25) at the end of Chapter 2 so that the teachers and district administrators cannot be identified. But the lesson is the same as Richard Ingersoll draws from his much larger surveys: Secondary science teachers are a hardy bunch. They love what they do, but there are limits to what they will tolerate from poor or indifferent administrators. And, given their value on the job market outside of education, school districts mistreat them at their peril.

Much more could be said. Much more might be recommended. But while there are more and more federal dollars going into America's schools and more and more federal influence upon them, the country remains committed to local control. Thus, we argue throughout this book, meaningful, lasting change in the quality of secondary science is going to depend on what teachers do for themselves. Our book, thanks to the amount of formal and informal input we have had from secondary science teachers themselves, is meant to be a resource for just that self-empowerment.

Avoiding Future Shortfalls:
Attracting and Keeping Gen Y in Teaching

"The existence of the 'lifetime teacher' can no longer be taken for granted," says Susan Moore Johnson, Harvard University professor of education. She finds that "the average teacher today expects to take on differing positions and responsibilities throughout his or her career" (Coggins 2008).

So, we should no longer expect a new teacher to continue for the next 30 years, but how about five years? Nearly half of all new teachers quit during their first five years, and the best and the brightest are often the first to leave. Schools in high poverty areas are particularly hard hit. Many of these are lower-performing schools and are under the gun to raise scores in math and reading or be shut down. They are often forced into exerting more heavy-handed control over what is taught in the classroom, driving new teachers out at an even faster rate (Viadero 2008).

One reason for their attrition is that new teachers are frequently given the most difficult and least desirable teaching assignments. Only two states, North and South Carolina, have policies that specifically reduce the workload for novice teachers in an effort to keep them in teaching (Chronister, Olson, and Bomster 2008). North Carolina allocates $1,000 for the mentoring of each new teacher. As new-teacher mentoring becomes more widely studied, this intervention may need to be expanded, because when districts don't invest in new-teacher programs, they pay later. It costs districts money to replace teachers who leave in their first few years, and students lose as well by not having the benefit of being taught by an experienced teacher.

According to a major study by the consulting firm Deloitte and Touche, recent college graduates, the 76 million members of the so-called Generation Y, are entering the job market with a new and different set of expectations. They want to work in a friendly environment, where they can continually gain new knowledge and skills. They are looking for challenges, and they like to solve problems. Most of all they want a job where they can have an impact—starting on Day One.

We just need to make them aware of how well teaching science fits their needs, and now more than ever we need to make some major changes in our schools to make teaching more attractive to this talented group of 21st-century workers.

One nontraditional approach has received a great deal of attention for its success in attracting a portion of Gen Y to teaching. The program, Teach for America, which began with a cohort of 500 in 1990, targets graduates from top colleges to commit to teach for two years in some of the nation's lowest-performing schools. The program has seen prodigious growth. In fall 2008, 24,700 applied for 3,700 teaching placements.

Like the students of the 1960s who were attracted to the Peace Corps—on which it can be said Teach for America is modeled—these young teachers are fast-tracked into their posts. They have five to six weeks of intensive training—with few of the traditional elements of teacher certification—and are assumed to be better-than-adequate teachers because they are well educated themselves.

On the one hand, Teach for America credits itself for elevating teaching as a profession because it is so selective. According to Jason Forrest, a member of the corps (those accepted into the program are called corps members), "Teach for America brands teaching in a way that makes it socially and professionally acceptable for top college graduates to be teachers." Indeed, for the 2008 corps, the average college GPA was 3.6. But, in reducing preservice training to a five-week intensive course, Teach for America has reaffirmed a common misperception that teaching is something anyone can do, with little or no training. This could be a giant step in devaluing the profession.

What matters to us is that Teach for America doesn't do much to solve the math/science teacher shortage. In 2008, fewer than 20% of the teaching corps came with math/science majors. Trying to rectify this imbalance, NASA, Amgen and other biomedical corporations are offering bonuses to math/science students willing to sign on with Teach for America. Time will tell if that proportion increases.

Even if Teach for America won't ever be a significant source of hard-to-find science and math teachers, exposing 20,000 high-achieving college graduates to classroom teaching has value. Nationwide, there are now 360 school leaders and 16 elected officials who got their start in Teach for America, the most famous of whom are Michelle Rhee, Washington, D.C.'s new chancellor of schools and Mike Feinberg and David Levin who colaunched a chain of 57 inner-city charter schools, collectively called the Knowledge is Power Program (KIPP).

One of the reasons Teach for America graduates may not stay in teaching over the long haul is that after two years, they discover that the system rarely offers the career growth, professional community, or performance-based compensation that they expect from a longer-term job. So, despite their positive experience in Teach for America, many "sit on the fence" regarding the longer-term commitment to teaching. From this perspective, researchers suggest we reframe teacher retention (Coggins 2008).

Reframing the teacher retention problem means defining a growth trajectory for teachers, including instructional leadership, team-based work, and differentiated pay, and one that rewards both longevity and excellence. It's time to find a way for teaching to live up to its potential as a profession that challenges and rewards practitioners. If we do not, our best young teachers will find the growth they seek outside the classroom.

Science Teaching as a **Profession**

References

Coggins, C. 2008. The post-boomer teacher crunch: Reframing "retention" to fit the needs of a new generation. *Education Week* (April 9): 1.

Committee on Prospering in the Global Economy of the 21st Century. 2007. *Rising above the gathering storm: Energizing and employing America for a brighter economic future.* Washington, DC: National Academies Press.

Editors. 2008. Grading the states' outcomes, policies. *Education Week* (January 10): 6.

Etzioni, A., ed. 1969. *The semi-professions and their organization.* New York: Free Press.

Gordon, R., T. J. Kane, and D. O. Staiger. 2006. *The Hamilton project: Identifying effective teachers using performance on the job.* Washington, DC: The Brookings Institution.

Guarino, C. M., L. Santibanez, and G. A. Daley. 2006. Teacher recruitment and retention: A review of the recent empirical literature. *Review of Educational Research* 76 (2): 173–208.

Ingersoll, R. M. 2000. *Turnover among mathematics and science teachers in the United States.* Paper prepared for the National Commission on Mathematics and Science Teaching for the 21st Century, Washington, DC.

National Science Board. 2007. *A national action plan for addressing the critical needs of the U.S. science, technology, engineering and mathematics education system.* Arlington, VA. National Science Foundation.

National Science Foundation. 2008. *Science and engineering indicators, 2008, volume 1.* Arlington, VA: National Science Foundation.

Rowland, R. 2007. *2003–04 Schools and Staffing Survey.* Washington, DC: National Center for Education Statistics.

Viadero, D. 2008. Working conditions trump pay: When it comes to retaining teachers, studies suggest that the circumstances of their jobs may matter even more than their salaries. *Education Week* (Jan 10): 1.

Chapter 2

Attrition:
Why It Matters

School reform cannot succeed unless it focuses on creating the conditions in which teachers can teach, and teach well.

(National Commission on Teaching & America's Future 1996)

The impetus for this book and for much of the nation's conversation during recent years about the impending "shortfall" of science teachers was the publication in 2007 of a National Academy of Sciences study, provocatively titled *Rising Above the Gathering Storm*. Basing their analysis on the numbers of existing and available science, technology, engineering, and mathematics (STEM) teachers, the authors called for an increase of 10,000 new science and mathematics teachers per year for the next decade to educate what they estimate to be "10 million minds" (Committee on Prospering in the Global Economy of the 21st Century 2007).

Studies by the National Academy are always taken seriously, but this time, even more so. For one thing, the number "10,000 per year" got widespread attention. It led many of the nation's well-meaning schools of education and supportive foundations to set about trying to figure out how to recruit, train, induct, and deliver the numbers.

The California State University system promised its governor it would double its output of science/math teachers. The University of California system (never a large producer) promised to triple its output, and the federal government weighed in with a new (and long overdue) set of financial aid packages (including Noyce scholarships as well as a variety of loan forgiveness plans) intended specifically for undergraduates with strong science or mathematics backgrounds, willing to consider teaching as a career.

Not every expert saw the impending shortfall as mainly a "production problem." Other researchers focused, rather, on teacher turnover—meaning the rate of departure of teachers from their teaching jobs. Richard Ingersoll and his colleagues at the Center for the Study of Teaching and Policy at the University of Pennsylvania reason that if as many as 50% of all new STEM teachers actually leave teaching within their first five years (only an estimate, not a statistic), and if they could be persuaded not to, then the United States would only have to produce half as many replacements, or 5,000 new science and math teachers per year (National Commission on Teaching & America's Future 2003).[1]

The Ingersoll group is not alone in trying to understand teacher turnover. State and local governments are very concerned about its costs. In June 2007, *Teacher Magazine* reported that, with some 17% of all teachers in all grade levels leaving teaching each year, teacher turnover is "spiraling out of control" and is now costing the United States from $4.9 to $7 billion per year (Palmer). These costs are derived from schools and school districts having to recruit, hire, and train replacement teachers.

To the many solutions offered to fix the problem (on-site mentoring, professional development, higher pay), we will argue in this book that improvements in the teacher's work life, including his or her empowerment vis-à-vis school officials and school boards, could make a substantial and permanent difference in the turnover rate.

If this is so, the first answer to the question of why it matters (that science teaching is not treated as a profession) is this: It is costing schools and school districts the highly trained people in fields they need most, and it is costing the state and the nation money to replace them!

Out-of-Field Teaching

The authors of *Rising Above the Gathering Storm* made much of the problem of out-of-field teaching, especially in the sciences and mathematics. Tracking teaching assignments by teachers' undergraduate majors, the report found that roughly 30% of teachers in grades 7–12 who teach one or more science classes did not have a minor in one of the sciences or in science education,

---

1. Not a far-fetched figure considering one-third of all new teachers leave the classroom within three years, and one-half within five years.

and 41% did not have a major or regular certification in one or more of the courses they were assigned to teach. Middle-school teachers (not covered in this book) and those working in inner-city schools demonstrate the worst fit between area of expertise and teaching assignment. Ingersoll and his colleagues in their *Out of Field Teaching Report* found similar patterns overall (Ingersoll 2003).

Ingersoll uses correlation to get at which variables (other than gross shortages) might impact out-of-field teaching. By connecting the percentages of out-of-field teachers with types and locations of schools, sizes of student body, and other variables, he concludes that the issue isn't simply inadequacy of preservice preparation (as was argued by the authors of *Rising Above the Gathering Storm*), but also in school misassignment. Here's the way his group explains their finding:

> The data show that those (secondary) teachers teaching out of field are not newcomers, but typically veteran teachers with 14 years experience, 45 percent of whom hold graduate degrees in disciplines other than the subject they have been assigned to teach.... Their misassignments typically involve one or two classes out of a typical normal day of five classes.... In a typical year some out-of-field teaching takes place in more than one-half of all U.S. secondary schools and one-fifth of the public's grades 7–12 teaching force does some out-of-field teaching. (Ingersoll 2003)

These statistics lead researchers to conclude that mandating more rigorous academic requirements for prospective teachers may not be enough to alleviate the shortage of trained teachers in science. So long as large numbers of teachers continue to be assigned to teach subjects other than those for which they were trained, these problems will continue. So the second question for policy makers to consider is why are so many teachers misassigned?

The problem isn't restricted to science (and math). Even in English and social studies, Ingersoll and his team of researchers find similar patterns of misassignment. But the issue is more serious in science. Like a foreign language, science is a specialty subject, requiring special training to teach well. Ingersoll and his team don't dismiss supply and demand entirely, but when they study school-to-school differences in the numbers of teachers teaching out of field, they conclude that "the way schools are organized and teachers are managed accounts for as much of the problem of out-of-field teaching as do inadequacies in teacher supply"(Ingersoll 2003, p. 22).

In short, school principals and other building-level supervisors have too much say in deciding who teaches what. Or to put it more bluntly, principals are not sufficiently accountable for the decisions they make about how teachers are employed and utilized. Here are examples of how this plays out:

- Rather than try to locate and hire a new science teacher for a state-mandated but underfunded program, a principal may choose an English or a social studies teacher to "cover" for a year.

- If a qualified science teacher leaves midsemester, the principal may hire a substitute (almost always a generalist) rather than search for a qualified replacement.

- When having to choose between doubling a class size (with a qualified teacher up front) or having two smaller classes with one taught by an unqualified teacher, the principal may choose the latter.

While teachers are subject to an elaborate array of state certification requirements designed to ensure their basic preparation and competence, there is too little accountability as to how teachers are employed and utilized once on the job. Most states allow local school administrators to bypass even the limited certification requirements that do exist.

This is why professionalizing teachers' work lives matters.

Two Ways of Dealing With the "Shortfall"

There are (at least) two ways of dealing with the current and future shortfall of science teachers in U.S. schools. One is to put a value on "new production," or as the authors of *Rising Above the Gathering Storm* would advise, turn out 10,000 new STEM teachers per year. Another—and these are not necessarily mutually exclusive solutions—is to better analyze and deal with the loss of teachers who have already been trained. If misassignment frustrates teachers and underserves their students, then misassignment has to be addressed—but so must overall attrition, the reasons teachers leave the school where they have been working and, in some cases, give up their profession altogether.

Teachers' Reasons for Leaving

In 2006, The Center for Teacher Quality in the Office of the Chancellor at California State University assigned Ken Futernick, then director of K–12 studies, to find and interview teachers in the California public school system who had left teaching during the previous five years. Futernick began with a wide sample, taking names from California's teacher retirement system. From 6,000 randomly selected K–12 teachers (not specific to science or math, nor to any particular grade level), Futernick found nearly half were thinking about leaving (or at least transferring to another school or school district). Focusing on those, he was able to solicit responses to his questionnaire and to do follow-up interviews with 875 teachers who were either

- no longer teaching in a California K–12 public school,

- planning to leave teaching altogether within the next two years, or

- trying to transfer away from their current school within the next two years.

The finding that matters to our analysis is that 29% of these teachers' reasons for leaving or transferring were related not only to poor compensation but also to working conditions, specifically "dissatisfaction with school conditions" (Futernick 2007).[2] These included what Futernick generalizes under the term *bureaucratic impediments* such as the following:

- Excessive testing and bookkeeping

- Overly scripted curriculum

- Poor administrative support

- Lack of local decision-making authority

- Lack of shared vision with the district

- Lack of resources including up-to-date textbooks and access to educational software

- Unsupportive principal (Futernick 2007)

Futernick's study did not focus specifically on secondary (math or) science teachers, but other studies have. The Teacher Follow-Up Survey (TFS) regularly undertaken by the National Center for Education Statistics finds that while math and science teachers leave a particular school at a lower rate than "other teachers" (in a single year 6% vs. 9%), they do so for different reasons:

- 29.4% to pursue a career other than teaching (compared with 25.5% for "other teachers")

---

2. Other reasons included their discovery that "teaching was not the right career choice for me" and the "negative public image of teachers."

- 25.3% for better salary and benefits (compared with 12.8% for "other teachers")

- 18% because of dissatisfaction with teaching as a career (compared with 14.1% for other teachers)

- 20.8% because of dissatisfaction with their school or teaching assignments (compared with 15.4% for other teachers) (National Center for Education Statistics 2008)

The Teacher Follow-Up Survey of math/science teacher-leavers deals with "school leadership" only indirectly. The phrases teachers select are "dissatisfaction with teaching as a career" and/or "dissatisfaction with their school or teaching assignments." But we found many science teachers agreed with Futernick's conclusion that school leadership plays a central role in teacher retention. Futernick puts it this way:

> Teachers want their principals to be effective instructional leaders, but they also want them to create safe and clean teaching environments where staff members are able to participate in decision making, where teachers have adequate time to collaborate and plan, and where unnecessary bureaucratic demands are minimized. (2007, p. 20)

How much of this kind of dissatisfaction shows up in other surveys? Or might Futernick's findings be specific to California? A study, also published in 2007, of Arkansas teachers of math, science, and computer science (most probably secondary, though this is not specified) who had or were contemplating quitting teaching for other jobs found (and teachers could choose more than one) low salaries (31%) and opportunities in other fields (21%) together accounted for only half of their reasons for leaving. Twenty-seven percent were leaving or would leave because of student discipline problems.

But for 25% of the would-be leavers, the problems were lack of administrative support. Excessive paperwork and hours accounted for 12%, and lack of teacher mentoring accounted for 9%. In our reading of these results, Arkansas teachers were leaving in large part because they were unable to affect those school policies that kept them from doing their jobs well (Arkansas News Bureau 2007).

For some teachers, "lack of administrative support" occurs at the school level; for others, at their district's central office. Other surveys, in multiple states (subject not specified), find that only one-third of teachers feel they are "centrally involved in school decision making" (Hirsch 2008, pp. 30–33). Futernick concludes of his own survey and his reading of others':

Teachers want to work in schools where they can thrive personally and professionally. And they're not going to thrive and extend themselves if they don't feel comfortable with their colleagues and the school leadership. Effective leaders create structures in which…teachers have a certain authority. (2007, p. 63)

The Power Matrix

To understand the locus of control in today's secondary science teachers' lives, we constructed a "power matrix" early in the development of our listening project. We asked an ever-expanding network of website respondents to answer the question, "Who decides what in your school?" by filling out our matrix. Here are their responses (from 100 respondents):

At your school, who makes decisions for the following? (Check all that apply):

	State	District	School Board	Principal	Science Chair	Teachers	Other (specify)
Pay	35	68	39	4	1		5 Union
Teaching assignments		12		95	59	8	
Class size	14	31	22	47	20	2	8 Counselors
Composition of class (type of students)	8	21	5	52	19	8	10 Counselors
Credential requirements	65	20	16	6	2		
Hiring new teachers	2	34	32	85	58	5	
Rewards for exemplary service	8	10	16	20	6		43 None
Budget for materials	10	43	40	92	33	2	
Professional development	14	43	20	69	20	17	
School calendar	13	48	61	21	1	11	

The cells in the matrix do not directly correlate to the number of correspondents because respondents often checked more than one decision maker and sometimes checked none.

We will be returning to this matrix again. For this first appraisal, notice how few of the crucial decisions affecting their work are nowadays made by the teachers!

The Critical Nexus: Leadership and Power

In this age of educational accountability, tests—often multiple-choice—are being used as the measure of schools' and teachers' effectiveness. But when these tests are designed by non–science teachers (even by nonteachers), and when the exam items fly in the face of inquiry-based science, then teachers lose one of the most fundamental aspects of professionalism: *the power to determine their own efficacy.* Though teachers may still design and administer classroom assessments, these results are dwarfed by the "all-important" state science tests.

Leadership at the building level is a critical factor in teacher retention, say experts on teacher attrition such as Futernick and Ingersoll. Effective leaders do not accrue power for its own sake. Rather, they create structures where teachers can take responsibility and exercise control. The respondents to our power matrix also reveal a significant appetite to have authority over (1) curriculum, (2) classroom assignments, and (3) student assessment. They are frustrated when that power is wrested from them. Ideally an administrator should be comfortable sharing decision making with teachers about critical areas of school management (Ingersoll 2006).

In the worst-performing schools, where teacher attrition is high (see the Close-Ups sidebar that begins on p. 25), power exists without leadership, and among the most talented science teachers—based on our respondents—leadership exists without power. The challenge is to align power and leadership in such a way that high-quality teaching and high-quality teachers can flourish.

What Science Teachers Say About Leaving

Rachel didn't leave teaching altogether, but she did resign her position at a large suburban district in the Northwest, and took a $15,000 pay cut to teach instead at a private Catholic high school. One reason was the curriculum notebook for sophomore chemistry she was handed when she first arrived. It described in lockstep mode what she had to teach. "There was a lesson prescribed for every benchmark on the state test," she explains. In her new position at the Catholic school, Rachel has been able to design her own chemistry curriculum and select the textbooks parents will buy for their children. The science budget is higher, and technology and other classroom resources are more plentiful. For these reasons, Rachel reports that she now feels supported in her role as a teacher. What she's saying is that control over curriculum—selection of textbooks and in-class examinations—are essential to her ability to exert power as a teacher.

Katie left a high-school science department because of burnout and now teaches in a community college. She explains her reason for leaving: "Good teachers are totally overworked and taken advantage of. You don't have time to do what you love, which is to create new lessons." The essence of her problem was that she had little personal control over her time.

In some schools, teachers are invited to sit on committees determining assessments, textbook adoptions, and curricula adoptions, but many of our informants complain they are not given time to do this work. Frustration over lack of power is not limited to science teachers or chairs. Amy is a science specialist in a fast-growing district in the Northwest. She serves 30 buildings in the district, focusing on secondary science, her specialty. Amy says she doubts many teachers leave because of pay. Rather, secondary science teachers need a different kind of compensation: recognition, support, relief regarding daily preps, and a sense that science in their school and state is a priority.

Conclusion

As our respondents reported to us in numerous ways, low pay, lack of autonomy, unstable working conditions, and an uncertain path to career advancement make science teachers feel like second-class citizens compared with other professionals.

One of many obstacles to change is that science educators work separately from one another more than most other professionals. Another barrier is the hectic, urgent everyday pace of school life. Each day is filled with scores of little fires to be put out. Parental concerns need to be mollified, students' health and discipline issues need to be addressed, and state and district regulations need to be met. In such a frantic climate, finding the time to reflect on the need for change and the energy to do something about this is rare. And, as is so often the case, this frenzied busyness is often mistaken for progress.

Yet another detractor to change is a culturally embedded compliance to authority. In schools, students and teachers alike are expected to respect authority, not to challenge it.

If, as is being documented, teachers are leaving the profession in record numbers, at special risk are science and math teachers who have the skill sets to land more lucrative and far more prestigious jobs outside of teaching.[3] The need for science and math teachers has become so critical that many

---

3. Data are scanty, but it is widely believed that secondary science teachers, even more than math teachers, are the single most highly sought professionals in business, government, and the independent sector, once they leave teaching.

states and school districts have to draft teachers into the classroom even before they complete their teacher preparation programs.

Teachers cite many reasons for leaving, but as we have found in our inquiries, school culture and lack of professional working conditions are always high on the list. Sixty-four percent of former teachers who took nonteaching jobs said they have more professional autonomy in their new positions than where they taught (Palmer 2007).

Our hypothesis corresponds to theirs: When teaching truly becomes a respected profession, schools will be able to attract many more academically qualified candidates and be able to retain experienced teachers as well.

With 14,000 school districts, all in true American fashion uniquely different, the question we faced as authors was how to determine a blueprint for change given the wide range of schools and school districts where science teachers work. Because there is no typical or average high school, how does one get a grip on the problem or the solution? One way—illustrated in the segment that follows—was to zero in not on the typical case, but instead on some best-case and worst-case scenarios. Each close-up provides some insights to help chart the direction we must proceed in order to stem the attrition of science and math teachers from secondary schools. Together, they remind us, as was so vividly documented in our power matrix, how important school leadership turns out to be.

Close-Ups

To put a local face on attrition, we will focus in this section on schools in two different regions of the United States. Each has taken a different tack to address the challenges of secondary science education with dramatically different results in teacher retention.

North Carolina

What brought us to North Carolina was the state's recognition that teacher attrition and the conditions that lead to attrition directly affect student learning. What distinguishes North Carolina from the pack is that it addresses teacher retention as integral to student achievement and to that end posits improved teacher working conditions as a goal of school reform.

North Carolina's two-term Governor Mike Easley was carrying on the tradition of dedication to educational issues in his state handed down by two governors before him: four-term Governor James Hunt, the man for whom the title "education governor" was first coined, and Governor Terry Sanford, who started the focus on education in North Carolina back when the state shared the bottom tier with Alabama.

North Carolina tries to make teachers more satisfied and more productive in two ways. In the public sector, it awards Real D.E.A.L. (Dedicated Educators Administrators and Learners)[4] status to schools that demonstrate both student achievement and excellence in working conditions. And with its math/science magnet academies, it relieves select public schools of all manner of state interference.

To understand just what constitute "excellent" working conditions for teachers at Real D.E.A.L. high schools, we traveled to an area of North Carolina known as the Research Triangle, home of some of the finest research universities (and some of the finest college basketball programs) in the nation. Here we interviewed teachers and administrators from the top math and science schools in the area. What follows are their stories.

Professional Autonomy at the School Level...

Tracy has commuted 88 miles round-trip for 15 years to teach at a suburban high school (we'll call RDHS), which was recently selected as a Real D.E.A.L. school finalist because of its student achievement and excellence in working conditions. Each day she passes several high schools, including one just three miles from her home, on her way to teach biology at her high school of nearly 2,500 students from varied economic and ethnic backgrounds.

Why?

"It's because of our school administration," Tracy explains. She is also the chair of the science department. "The principal is here for the teachers," adds Sarah, a chemistry/AP chemistry teacher who has taught science for 26 years (seven at RDHS) and plans to teach at least another 10 years. Like Tracy, the teachers we interviewed feel they have a voice in decisions made at the school level and, as a result, there is true consideration for teacher time. That translates into fewer required preps and more time for collaboration.

Ann, who is pregnant, has taught biology and chemistry at this impeccably clean high school for four years and has every intention to come back after her baby is born. She feels much more respected at RDHS than she did at the high school where she taught previously. And what she means by respect is this: "They

---

4. Real D.E.A.L. schools are selected using feedback from the Teacher Working Conditions Survey.

respect my time, and do not waste it with useless meetings and extra duties."

"Our principal wants us in the classroom. He wants us preparing the next lesson. And that's what we want," Tracy adds.

Another dimension of teachers' increased professional status at Tracy's school derives from schoolwide professional learning communities (PLCs, see Chapter 6). When a decision affecting the school community needs to be made, it is first sent to a teacher-run learning community for review. Learning communities also share the latest teaching methods and bring the newest technology tools to others in their own departments.

"Meetings are short. The teachers get right down to the nitty-gritty because they have other things to do, and they need to get back to their teaching, too," Sarah says, adding, "We are professional enough to respect one another's time."

...But Not at the District, State, or Federal Level

However generous and responsive their own school administration, state standards and state-mandated tests are having a major impact on what the science teachers teach, and on their ability to be creative. There's some resentment. "A lot of people who have never taught science are trying to tell us teachers how to teach," Tracy says.

And there's bitterness. State-mandated End-of-Course (EOC)[5] tests have changed the spirit of the school. Sarah, the chemistry teacher, remarks that the tests have taken on even more significance since they were folded into No Child Left Behind.

Another intrusion by state-level mandates is in the start date for school, intended to accommodate the tourist-driven economy at the North Carolina coast. The new calendar pushes final exams to after Christmas break and, worse

yet, gives Advanced Placement (AP) students less time to prepare for their May exams.

As far as teacher advancement is concerned, teachers at RDHS are especially fortunate. North Carolina is where National Board Certification began (see Chapter 6). Today the state offers teachers who get National Board Certification a 12% pay increase in most regions.

Freedom From State Mandates Allows for a Professional Culture

Down the road is a residential magnet school for 11th- and 12th-grade students with strong aptitude and interest in math and science.[6] Now 15 years old, the school was separately chartered by the governor as one of 10 state-based math and science magnet schools intended to address the need for more technically skilled workers so as to attract more high-tech industry to the state. Ask the school's chancellor why his teachers rarely leave except to retire, and he says it's because he transformed the culture of the school and made the faculty feel like valued leaders.

Ask Melissa, dean of science, a title she finds a bit pretentious, or any of the science teachers in her department, and they will say, "It's the students." What about the private office with a direct phone line that each teacher is given? And what about the lab technician who directs the student workers in setting up and breaking down labs and demonstrations?

"Nope, it's the students!"

"We make sure that no teacher takes a pay cut when they come here," reports the vice chancellor for academic programs. Indeed, teachers at the magnet school receive salaries on par with the state's highest salary scale.

---

5. EOC tests have been in place in North Carolina since the early 1980s and predate the NCLB accountability mandates.

6. Started in 1998, the magnet academy is a founding member of the National Consortium for Specialized Secondary Schools of Mathematics, Science and Technology whose mission is to attract and academically prepare students to be leaders in math and science. As of 2006, there were 80 schools serving more than 35,000 students.

Each teacher also receives a personal laptop computer to use on or off the totally wireless campus.

Open teaching positions arise not from teacher attrition but from expansion of the student body. And every opening attracts 20–30 applicants.

"We have a great job, because we have great students," says Melissa, who has taught chemistry for 18 years. Asked if she plans to continue teaching at this high school, she responds, "Goodness, yes!"

Melissa also teaches AP chemistry and oversees a student research program that is consistently represented in some of the most coveted scholarship awards and competitions in the United States. She also teaches a televised course with a Duke University pharmacology professor that integrates high-school chemistry and biology in the study of drugs and drug abuse. Melissa clearly sees herself as a professional and her school administrators as "folks that work for me." Her only complaint is that there is not enough time built into the day for collaboration with other teachers, but she feels that she and her science department enjoy a lot of autonomy in what they teach.

One benefit of teaching at this magnet school, as we have already noted, is that the school is exempt from the state-mandated tests, textbooks, and credentialing. "One of the most farsighted things we did was not put the school under the North Carolina state educational system," boasts the school chancellor. "This gives our teachers much greater flexibility in what they teach."

Indeed, decisions made about the curriculum, the school calendar, and bell schedule start in professional learning communities that are made up of faculty, staff, and administrators.

In North Carolina, the ground was fertile for improving science education. The state has created incentives for schools that reward teachers with reasonable workloads, sufficient time for planning and collaboration, and a voice in school governance. In our less-than-perfect world, even Real D.E.A.L. schools still face state tests that constrain teaching and learning, a school calendar dictated by convenience rather than curriculum, and limited career advancement opportunities. But still the schools thrive. They have become successful microcosms, providing teachers the opportunity to truly teach—which is what the most gifted teachers really want and what true professionals in any field desire.

Where—as in the math–science academy—there are exemptions from state testing, state-mandated textbook adoptions, and low teacher salaries, teachers make the decisions affecting their classrooms, most particularly curriculum. And they are provided the tools they need for excellent teaching.

In both cases, we see a harmonious alignment between science teachers and their administrators. This is not often the case in other schools around the country.

Somewhere in the Southwest: Exception, Anomaly, or Portent?

Science teachers travel from all over the United States to teach in this sunny, southwestern suburb. This community, like so many in the area, is growing at an exponential pace. During the past 25 years, the small farms and ranches that supported the 30,000 residents who lived here in the 1980s have been bulldozed to make room for the current population of nearly 250,000.

One high school served the community for 75 years, but during the past 10, three new high schools were built in attempts to keep pace with what has become one of the fastest-growing school districts in the nation. Lured by the promise of excellent salaries and benefits, and brand new high schools equipped with state-of-the-art labs, teachers leave their snow shovels and ice scrapers behind to live and work in this tidy, manicured, family-friendly community.

This well-funded, rapidly growing school district, a self-proclaimed "science Mecca," should by all rights be our poster child for the very best place for science teachers to work. Yet, we are told by the teachers we interview that it is, instead, one of the worst.

What makes this school district, flush with a steady stream of funding from a fast-growing population, fail its teachers? After all, it offers the most competitive salary packages in the state and some of the finest facilities.

What is wrong with this district is what is wrong with the direction that many of our school districts are heading. What follows is a cautionary tale, told to discourage others from following the same path.

No Oasis for Teachers

"I guess I should have known there was something wrong (with the 3,500–student high school) when I started the new school year with 70 other new hires (a more than 40% turnover)," says Katie, a biology teacher, who left the district after 12 years of teaching for a job selling Mary Kay products.

Susan, a former chemistry teacher who left the district after only three years for a pharmaceutical career, explains that she always wanted to be a teacher. "I was the kid who forced all the neighborhood kids to play school, and I was always the teacher." Hired straight out of college, Susan fully expected to teach the rest of her life. But after just one year in the district, she knew that she needed to find a new career.

Cathy, another biology teacher, came to the district from the Midwest where she taught for 13 years with her husband, a math teacher. They are going back as soon as the school year is over. "I never thought the education system could be so different from state to state," she says, adding, "This school district saps the life out of being a teacher."

Here are some of the reasons we were given for the district's failure to thrive: "They built a brand new school with no input from science teachers. The science labs have no sinks, hoods without ventilation, and carpet on the floors," says Barb, a former Earth and space science teacher now working at Starbucks. Worse even than the poor facilities are what the teachers call micromanagement around pupils' achievement on high-stakes tests.

From the science teachers' point of view, those who left and those who stayed, the district administrators are obsessively focused on showing student achievement gains on tests mandated by No Child Left Behind. So much so, that they have completely taken over much that the teachers used to do on their own.

Teachers have little to no input into the curriculum in their content area, or even what subject they will be assigned to teach. The curriculum is developed at the district level, as are the quarterly benchmark tests given to students. New teachers, usually fresh out of teachers' colleges, are hired with little input from teachers in the science department.[7] Teachers report a move in the district to make all the high schools (there are four) the same—offer the same classes, conform to the same schedule, and cover the curriculum with the same sequence of topics. As this plan unfolds, teachers are finding that fewer decisions are being made even by their own principals and more and more by the district with even less input from classroom teachers.

"I never got that good, happy feeling about teaching [on this job]. It was always this is our way, and you will teach our way," says Susan, the former chemistry teacher. She now claims to enjoy more autonomy and a great deal more respect as a pharmacist for a large chain of drug stores.

---

7. A serious problem when one considers that most building administrators (principals) are not themselves trained in science; nor have they ever taught science.

There's a strong assumption in this school district: If the students are not learning, the teacher must be doing something wrong.

Inappropriate Teacher Evaluation

One of the most troubling practices of this district is that evaluation of science teachers is entirely in the hands of administrators who have little or no background in science. Yet it is they who hire, fire, and evaluate science teachers districtwide.

This is why—or so it appears to the science teachers we interviewed—the principals, vice principals, and district representatives focus their evaluations on classroom management, and not on the delivery of the science content. As a former National Science Teachers Association (NSTA) official puts it, speaking of another set of administrators, "They don't know enough science to evaluate science instruction."[8] That's the problem.

Teachers not following the step-by-step procedure of instruction mandated by the district receive negative evaluations. And any negative evaluation will not only prevent a teacher from advancing on the career ladder, losing salary increments, but also can result in an unfavorable teaching assignment—teaching multiple subjects in multiple classrooms, for example, in the following year.

Although teachers may be evaluated as many as seven times in two weeks, principals are never evaluated by their staff. Nor, despite the fact that more and more high-school science teachers are leaving the district each year, have any of the "leavers" been given exit interviews.

"I am constantly amazed when I talk to teachers from my old district and tell them I am working at Starbucks. Their response is, 'Good for you,'" Barb says, adding she feels

8. Gerald F. Wheeler, NSTA executive director emeritus, personal communication to the authors.

much more valued by Starbucks than she ever felt as a high-school science teacher.

Katie, who now sells Mary Kay products, first tried teaching in a junior high school for a while after leaving the high school. There she found a supportive principal who allowed her much more freedom in the classroom. After the school posted low math and language arts scores, however, the principal was obliged to insist that she and the rest of the teachers incorporate language arts and math objectives into their science curriculum. During her last year, Katie had to pick up even more teaching objectives that the physical education department did not want to teach.

Carol and her husband are returning to the Midwest, where they will endure the "crappy weather" for the opportunity to teach at the same high school—a privilege they were not permitted in the Southwest district they are leaving. They will have smaller classes and expect to work in a more collaborative environment.

Susan has been a pharmacist for CVS for three years, where, she says, "My time is my own. I have a great support team and I absolutely feel more professional." Sadly, Susan wanted to be a teacher for as long as she can remember, but she vows she will never return to the profession. If it were just low pay or lack of respect, Susan explains, "I would probably still be there, but the combination is intolerable." "I'm done," she says.

How to Succeed in the District

Kelly, who describes herself as the "district golden child," has taught there for two years. She teaches 190 students during her seven-period school day (most teachers teach six periods). "I think it was three weeks before the end of school when I finally got to know their names," she said, adding, "I doubt I will get done with my grading by the end of the school year."

Kelly also spends two hours each day contacting parents and documenting her efforts in a communication log for her evaluators. Why did Kelly accept such a punishing schedule?

"Teachers who do not volunteer do not get the good classes to teach."

Kelly tells her story at a large round table in a restaurant where we have chosen to meet with a group of teachers because it's outside the district. The veteran teachers nod to one another making silent wagers on how long this bright, energetic young teacher will last under these conditions.

This district and the principals in the district convey distrust of the teachers' judgment by denying them a voice in decisions critical to classroom effectiveness. By providing insufficient support and ignoring inequities in power, the district and its teachers do not work together. Resentments thrive. Teacher initiative disappears. Thus, it is not simply whether teachers are well paid or how well schools are doing on state tests. The more important factor is whether teachers' working conditions support excellent teaching and teacher retention.

References

Arkansas News Bureau. 2007. Survey, Math/Science, Computer Teachers Most Likely to Quit for Other Jobs. September 13.

Committee on Prospering in the Global Economy of the 21st Century. 2007. *Rising above the gathering storm: Energizing and employing America for a brighter economic future.* Washington, DC: National Academies Press.

Futernick, K. 2007. *A possible dream: Retaining California teachers so all students learn.* Sacramento: The Center for Teacher Quality, California State University.

Hirsch, E. 2008. Empowering teachers. *Teacher Professional Development Sourcebook* Spring: 30–33.

Ingersoll, R. M. 2003. *Out of field teaching and the limits of teacher policy.* Seattle: University of Washington, Center for the Study of Teaching and Policy, September.

Ingersoll, R. M. 2006. *Who controls teachers' work? Power and accountability in America's schools.* Cambridge, MA: Harvard University Press.

National Center for Education Statistics. 2008. Attrition of public school mathematics and science teachers. *Issue Brief* (May): 3.

National Commission on Teaching & America's Future. 1996. *What matters most: Teaching for America's future.* New York: National Commission on Teaching & America's Future.

National Commision on Teaching & America's Future. 2003. *No dream denied: A pledge to America's children.* Summary report. Washington, DC: National Commission on Teaching & America's Future.

Palmer, K. 2007. Why teachers quit. *Teacher Magazine* (May 1). Also available online at *www.edweek.org*

Chapter 3

How Did Teaching First Gain and Then Lose Its Professional Status?

Perhaps more than any other religion, the Jewish faith extends to the teacher and the act of teaching its highest, holiest, status. *Rabbi* is in fact the ancient Hebrew word for "teacher" and the young (men, in the old days) who were selected for "study" were exempted (as were their teachers) from heavy labor. The same is true of the Islamic teachers in the Madrasses all over the Middle East. And until 1862 when the Morrill Act gave grants of public land to educators for the purpose of establishing "land-grant" universities, teacher/ministers were the bedrock of American higher education.

But what about "lower" education? What can we learn about teaching as a profession from its history? Public school teaching is characterized in the United States by a longstanding concern for local control. Into the mix historically came politics (anti-Intellectualism, Progressivism, and anti-Progressivism), and added to all of that, the perception of teaching based on women's overall low employment status in prior centuries.[1]

---

1. The following discussion is based on wide reading in the field, but the interpretations and conclusions are the authors' own. See, for example, Cremin (1961), Butts and Cremin (1953), and Lieberman (1956).

Long before the American Revolution, elementary-school teaching—especially in the towns and villages—was the province of women. Women ran the "Dame Schools" during the colonial period and continued to teach the very young through the 19th century.

Meanwhile, in rural areas, farm men often did the teaching, especially of young boys, during the off-season when there was no farming to do. Women would then fill in during the summer, when the older boys, along with farmers and farmhands, were too busy with planting and harvesting to go to school. But in both settings, rural and town, teachers were expected to maintain discipline and drill the required subject skills (basic reading, writing, and arithmetic) that a frontier economy required.

Wherever they worked, however, teachers were revered and respected by the children they taught and, because they had to be unmarried to teach, cared for by the communities they served. But was teaching thought to be a "profession?" Here the story is a little murky.

Teachers taught students but were employed by whoever raised the money to manage the schools. Historians of education see this as generating a constant tension between control (by the school administrator, the school superintendent, and a school board of citizens) and the autonomy of the teacher's role in the classroom. Some of this tension remains.

Public school systems as we know them today only began to emerge between the Revolutionary War and the Civil War. But just when the growth of public schools might have regularized the training and credentialing of teaching, President Andrew Jackson (in the 1830s) took an opposite tack. In an excess of democratization of the American polity, his position was that any citizen had the qualifications for holding any public office. This, at a time when a teacher had only to have completed one year more of schooling than the pupils she taught. (Teacher training would not begin in earnest until after the Civil War.) So Jackson's lack of appreciation for the skills required to teach encouraged schools to continue to hire young, unskilled women, who were both cheap and easy to control.

Essential to any profession is agreed-upon training and credentialing. And this took longer to achieve for teachers in the United States than elsewhere. In fact, the idea of a "normal" (teacher training) institution had to be imported—from Prussia and from France. And as normal schools proliferated, they were, not surprisingly, attacked for being "foreign." Little by little, the idea took hold that there was something to study in preparation for teaching. But it was decades before a majority of public school teachers received even a year or two of pedagogical training.[2]

The first so-called normal school opened in Lexington, Massachusetts, in July 1839; the second, two months later. Nevertheless, by the time of the outbreak of the Civil War, 20 years after the founding of the first school, there were still only 12 such schools in the country. But at least there were two training manuals in widespread use: David Page's *Theory and Practice of Teaching* and Samuel Hall's *Lectures in Schoolkeeping* (an interesting term, perchance related to "housekeeping?"). By 1892, there was sufficient interest in the "science" of teaching to cause the founding of Teacher's College in association with Columbia University of New York (Stinnett 1968).[3]

But just as normal schools were providing teachers with training befitting a profession, enthusiasm for "scientific management"—which would soon undermine teachers' autonomy—was sweeping the country. By 1917, the principalship and the superintendency were institutionalized and the new superintendents began to treat teachers as "industrial workers" to "execute" plans developed by the central office and to be "managed" by the men who moved into school and district administration. To what extent this was expected to mirror the power relations in the patriarchal family is a matter of speculation (Lortie 1969). But male or female, the teacher-as-employee with the school board and its designate the school superintendent-as-employer characterize present-day relations.

It is interesting that teachers have rarely contested the right of persons outside the occupation to govern their work. Scholars of education note that even teacher associations appear to accept the relations between teachers and principals, and teachers and superintendents, as relations between employees and employers. The two main associations of teachers, about which we will have more to say in Chapter 5, reflect the schism. The National Education Association (NEA) is made up of both teachers and their managers, so it would not be likely for that association to challenge the structure of public schools. Meanwhile, the American Federation of Teachers (AFT), a union

2. The reluctance to regularize and professionalize was not limited to education in the United States. It took even longer to set entrance and curriculum and credentialing standards in medicine and in law.

3. T. M. Stinnett, a historian of American education, dates the first round of teacher professionalization with the adoption of teacher prep academies by collegial institutions, like Columbia's. In 1900, there were 300 so-called normal schools exclusively for teacher training, not able to award baccalaureate degrees. These slowly transformed themselves in the next two decades into degree-granting teachers' colleges on the model of Columbia's, and by 1967 few single purpose teacher-training institutions remained. In that same period, states began to require a bachelor's degree for teachers at all levels.

that excludes principals and superintendents from its membership, has chosen to concentrate on issues of money and working conditions, not on the right of citizen boards (or, in the blatant case of No Child Left Behind, the federal government) to control instruction.

The lesson we authors take from the history of public education in the United States is this: Whatever their expectations of professionalism may be, neither teachers nor those who represent them have so far effectively challenged the power relations that govern schools (Lortie 1969). How much this affects secondary science teachers' self-image, their power, their working conditions, and their autonomy at work is what we will continue to explore in this book and, at the end (see Chapter 9), recommend that we change.

Adding Science to the Curriculum

For a very long time, science and other of the "useful arts" were not part of any public school curriculum, neither in colonial times, nor after the country became a republic. Their first appearance (thanks to initial efforts by none other than Benjamin Franklin) were in private, coeducational academies—not the public schools—where tuition-paying pupils learned geography, natural history, health, astronomy, and agronomy, in addition to English, history, and "arithmetic." The academies proliferated and by 1850 were the dominant form of precollege education in the United States with 6,000 pupils (of both sexes) registered. As the first teaching institutions to offer courses in sciences, the offerings were said to be very uneven, with many instructors underprepared (Ireton 2001).

With this background, at the close of the 19th century, the National Education Association's so-called Committee of Ten met in 1892 to establish a norm for the types of science courses public schools should offer. Made up largely of college and university professors, the Committee of Ten assumed pupils studying science were all college bound. Nonetheless, they came up with a minimum requirement—that 25% of the curriculum be devoted to the sciences—and a pattern that persists well into our era: Grade 9, physical geography (now Earth sciences); Grade 10, biology; Grade 11, chemistry; Grade 12, physics (Ireton 2001).

This was no ordinary "committee" but rather a multifaceted initiative. The Committee of Ten—itself comprised of 10 educators, chaired by Charles Eliot, then president of Harvard University—created nine further conference committees, of which three were in the sciences, divided, interestingly enough, into (1) physics, astronomy, and chemistry; (2) natural history; and (3) geography. In 1894, their recommendations were made public (Sheppard and Robbins 2007).

What's interesting for our generation of teachers is that the Committee of Ten turned its back on "science for the elite" and chose, instead, a "citizen-science" approach. Their argument was that all students should have the rigorous mental training that the study of science provides, instead of a few learning a preprofessional science curriculum. This earlier version of "Science for All Americans" extended to laboratory work, for which the committee actually proposed a list of specific experiments.

This meant secondary science teachers had to be particularly well educated in science with the capacity to teach and to do lab science. This in turn gave science teachers a special shared identity, separate even from mathematics, and much motivation to converge and consult with one another in educational organizations such as the National Science Teachers Association.

The next big national thrust with regard to science education in the schools came 63 years after 1894, immediately following the Soviets' successful launching of the first Earth-orbiting satellite, Sputnik, in 1957. The Soviets' sudden advantage in space had implications for the military as well as for science. It is no exaggeration to say that Sputnik caused a tsunami of concern among U.S. policy makers and massive investment in new advanced curricula, teacher retraining at government expense, and generous science scholarships for any able (usually male) student willing to study science, mathematics, or engineering. That story has been told elsewhere and often.

More recently, in 1996, responding to a new cycle of multinational tests that revealed U.S. pupils were not competitive internationally, the National Academy of Sciences produced a new set of National Science Standards (see *www.nap.edu/openbook.php?record_id=4962*). As every science teacher knows, the new standards were supposed to incorporate teaching by inquiry rather than memorization, which would have made the curriculum much less amenable to multiple-choice testing. How No Child Left Behind (NCLB)—the Third Revolution—will test science knowledge is about to be divulged.

Deprofessionalizing Teaching

It's probably overstated but there seems to be a race to *deprofessionalize* public school teaching. We trace the first salvo to a 1969 collection of scholarly essays by some of the nation's most eminent sociologists (not long after sociology itself had to struggle to earn academic recognition in the United States). The book is titled *The Semi-Professions and Their Organization: Teachers, Nurses, Social Workers* (Etzioni 1969). The fact that all three of the so-named "semi" professions under scrutiny were (and to a large extent remain) female dominated was not lost on the sociologists of that day. But because the scholars were operating prior to the second wave of feminism, they were much less careful about projecting their own personal prejudice about women as a lesser caste than they would have been a decade later.[4]

It is striking to a present-day reader how much their sexism colors their analysis. Here's what they write about the "semi-professions:"

Compared to doctors, lawyers, and priests, the semi-professions fail to display those characteristics associated with the professions:

- Their training is shorter,

- Their status is less legitimated,

- Their right of "privileged communication" is less well established,

- They control less of a specialized body of knowledge, and [most importantly]

- They have less autonomy from supervision and societal control. (Etzioni 1969, p. v)

The authors are quick to say they could have chosen a more derogatory term, such as *sub-professions* or *pseudo-professions*. And they admit they might "arouse some resentment" among the millions of people who work in these semi-professions "for we do not accept some of the claims and self-images these professions have fostered." Indeed, the "problem" the author/sociologists see is exactly the impetus for *our* work:

> A significant segment of the semi-professions aspire to a full-fledged professional status and sustain a professional self-image, despite the fact that they themselves are often aware that they do not deserve such a status, and ... they objectively do not qualify as semi-professionals see it, they are more than secretaries, salesgirls, or office clerks.... Not wishing to be identified with the lower-status group, they cling to the higher aspiration of being a full professional.

Rather than try to "pass (the authors actually use the term *pass*) for what they are not," the authors recommend that these middle-class groups

---

4. This is an opinion of the authors, one of whom is a historian of Feminism's Second Wave (see Tobias 1997).

acknowledge (accept) their position as semi-professionals rather than seek to improve their status (Etzioni 1969).[5]

We don't agree. And we think most teachers wouldn't agree either.

To be sure, some of the parameters of a teacher's work life cannot be altered. Except in the private school sector (and even there teachers are managed by those who pay for their children's tuition), teachers are inevitably employed by local boards and managed by school administrators and superintendents. But if one identifies the 12 critical elements of professional life, as we do (see The Elements of the Profession sidebar that begins on p. 41) we believe some positive changes can be made in teachers' work lives, and in their status as professionals.

Even more than in 1969 (12 years post-Sputnik) when Etzioni and his coauthors first offered the "semi-professions" as a description of teaching, the nation, and its economy, is wholly dependent on high-quality schooling for its young. Because we are especially short of teachers in subjects such as secondary science and mathematics, we must ask teachers what's missing from their work life, and find ways to provide it.

Our Findings

There is no question in our minds and in the minds of the teachers contacted over the past two years that teaching is a profession, or that it could be one if reforms are implemented. Secondary science teachers especially appreciate their relative autonomy, job security, working for a higher calling, and the opportunity for originality and creativity in their classrooms. But at the same time they cite a lack of respect in the community; inadequate wages and opportunities for advancement; limited mobility; and too little time set aside for research, professional development, self-improvement, and collaboration.

To be sure, when we question teachers regarding their perceived professional status, even while they bemoan their salaries, many of our interviewees find the privileges and the perks of teaching (vacation time, autonomy, self-regulation) to more than offset the lower pay. For most, the missing element continues to be time, time enough to do the job "right."

What Science Teachers Say About Why They Teach

There is widespread agreement among our informants that science teaching is more than a career; it is a "calling." "What hooks us into doing science is

---

5. Not all the "semi-professions" are dominated by women, the authors concede, though only nursing, teaching, and social work are the subject of this book. They define engineers as "semi-professionals," too.

discovery," says Lynn, adding, "We live for the moment when you see something you've never seen before." Comparable to the "lightbulb" experience in discovery, Lynn lives for the moment "when a student suddenly gets a piece of knowledge for the first time, or in a new way."

Bea, a first-year teacher who migrated from another field in what she refers to as the real world, writes, "For the most part, I'm my own judge as to how well I do each day, given the time and materials available to me. Having been in the 'real' world, and much less in control." Another career switcher observes, "I enjoy teaching chemistry because I'm a far better teacher than I was a researcher."

What gets in the way of this pleasurable pursuit of challenges and discovery? Even among those who do not plan to leave teaching, there are frustrations. Rick, who is in his 20th year of teaching, writes, "What makes me feel unprofessional are government mandates, the administration of my school, parents, and students who all want me to lower my standards."

Safety issues often stretch a science teacher's sense of ethical responsibility. At one school, where one of our informants was working, all science teachers were required to be trained in chemical hygiene. When asked to sign off that they had received this training (they had not), the teachers refused. They recognized, correctly, that they would be sued in case of student injury and asserted their rights to protect the students, the school, and themselves. Their responsible self-regulation was highly professional.

Becky's post reveals she is permitted to write her own curriculum and feels very much as if she's her own boss in the classroom. Steve, on the other hand, feels he is too little "accountable." "My only task," he writes, "is to turn in my syllabus at the beginning of the semester, and my grades at the end."

All teachers highly value whatever independence remains to them after state-mandated testing has taken away many of their other functions. Reports George on our website, "Teaching is a job that allows me to use a lot of different abilities." Ed from Connecticut and Jamie describe themselves in almost the same way, as "eduholic," loving to learn, to teach, and to learn about teaching.

The Elements of the Professions

A professional must have control over his or her conditions of practice.[6]

History teaches us much about the professions. Almost as early as the birth of civilization, three professions (often preceded by the term *learned*) were acknowledged as necessary, valuable, and different in essential ways from mere work. These were medical doctors, lawyers, and priests. Regulated and legitimized by the locale in which they lived, these men (they were always and only men) were licensed to carry out what were considered socially useful tasks on behalf of the state or the church. Medicine, law, and the priesthood all involve major functions of society, all are fraught with risks to the health and well-being of individuals, and all require (as much then as now) approved academic training. The reason these functions had to be regulated by society and the reason they were provided with special incentives and rewards is that they intrude on personal autonomy:

- The power to intervene in a person's body (medical doctors)

- The power to intercede in a person's financial and property relationships (lawyers)

- The power to regulate a person's behavior (priests and ministers)

Over time, the professions have both expanded and evolved, providing material for us to draw from as we ponder the state of secondary science teaching as a profession. And so we can begin to ask, What are the elements of a profession? What makes someone a "professional" as opposed to an employee? Or a manager? Or an artist?

6. Judith Ramaley, president, Winona State University, Minnesota, personal communication to the authors.

We are not the first to ask these questions. Back in the 1960s, the National Education Association produced "The Yardstick of a Profession" for teachers, which listed the following (somewhat idealized) characteristics:

- A profession involves activities essentially intellectual.

- A profession commands a body of specialized knowledge.

- A profession requires extended professional (as contrasted with general) preparation.

- A profession demands continuous in-service growth.

- A profession affords a life career and permanent membership.

- A profession sets up its own standards.

- A profession exacts service above personal gain.

- A profession provides a strong, closely knit, professional organization (National Association of Teachers, as quoted in Stinnett 1968).

What we found missing from this classic list were elements that kept coming up in our interviews, in the power matrix we devised (see p. 21), and in responses to questions on our website. The science teachers whom we queried (and others who wrote spontaneously to us, once they learned we were doing this research) had issues with autonomy and control; with earnings and status vis-à-vis not just society as a whole, but also with their building administrators, the school superintendent, the local and state authorities who set standards, and the federal government (insofar as it sets standards and measures teacher quality). Portability of benefits and status matter to them, as does mobility in all its aspects.

So, building on previous statements, we amended the NEA's essential elements of the profession to suit secondary science teachers in the following way:

1. **Knowledge-based expertise that derives from academic training**
   Professionals are tested for entry and for continued competence. As with other professions such as law and medicine, teaching requires university-level degree attainment, an internship followed by testing for certification in the areas of subject matter knowledge, and expertise in pedagogy.

2. **Code of ethical behavior (on and off the job)**
   Essential to the job of teaching is modeling the highest standards of ethical behavior, both in the classroom and in the community.

3. **A moral commitment embodied in a public service (beyond the desire for profit)**
   Teaching, and teaching science even more so, involves a moral commitment to the wider community. Anyone qualified to teach science in high school could make much more money in the private sector. For those trained in science who choose, instead, to teach, teaching is a calling.

4. **Higher-than-average standard of living**
   Income advantages to the profession of teaching are being eroded as the business world offers more opportunities for science-trained professionals (especially women who previously might never have considered options other than teaching, nursing, and social work). Many (see Chapter 5, on pay) are calling for pay plans that offer higher salaries to math and science teachers to bring educators' yearly pay closer to those of jobs in the private sector.

5. **Autonomy—standards defined and policed by the profession**
   This is an area in serious need of change. Too many decisions about what is done in the classroom are made by people who never set foot in a classroom. Science teachers have very little say in the important decisions made on hiring, evaluation of teachers, school policies, schedules, and class size. More importantly, teachers are starting to lose control over what and how they teach and how they are assessed.

6. **Mobility (including portable benefits) that make it possible for the professional to be independent of a particular employer**
   Teachers' benefits and salary scale are usually locked into the district or school where they are employed. Teachers moving from state to state quite often have to reapply and retest for certification. Most states only compensate teachers arriving from another state for a limited number of years of experience putting newly arrived teachers back at the bottom of the career ladder.

7. **High status in the minds of ordinary citizens; respect of parents, supervisors, and society**
   Status in the United States is linked to salary, so teachers' social status is quite low. Another measure in the public eye are failing test scores, and failing students are being presented to the public, at least by some critics, as a direct result of failing teachers.

8. **Career advancement/job security**
   There is little room for career advancement in teaching beyond the salary ladder that rewards seniority and levels of education.

While tenure protects teachers from unwarranted dismissal, teachers who lose favor with administrators often find themselves facing intolerable teaching assignments that force them to resign.

9. **Time set aside for collaboration, research, professional development, and self-improvement**
One thing teachers have less of than money is time. Yet, secondary science teachers need time to keep current with rapid developments in their fields; also to connect with the larger community of scientists to stay relevant and build relationships that will inevitably improve their practice. (See Chapter 7 on associating science teachers with the wider world of science.)

10. **Input regarding federal/state/local policy**
Traditionally teachers have had little influence on educational policy, local, state, or federal. They are called on (required) to implement these policies (e.g., write questions along prescribed outlines for high-stakes science tests) but not to debate the scripts or timetables for those tests. (See Chapter 9 for some new avenues for teacher input.)

11. **Support staff**
Teachers are finding their time is being spent less and less on teaching and more and more on paperwork and other non-teaching tasks that could be done by staff assistants. Among these tasks are what teachers called "administrivia": printing, photocopying, and materials preparation.

12. **Professional leave time**
Most science teachers point to national and regional science-teaching conferences as the single most important way through which they can improve their teaching both in terms of pedagogy and content. Nonetheless, attending these conferences is becoming increasingly difficult. Few districts provide funds for teacher travel and for the teacher replacement required.

References

Butts, R. F., and L. Cremin. 1953. *History of education in American culture*. New York: Henry Holt.

Cremin, L. 1961. *The transformation of the school: Progressivism in American education 1876–1957*. New York: Alfred Knopf.

Etzioni, A. ed. 1969. *The semi-professions and their organization: Teachers, nurses, social workers*. New York: Free Press.

Ireton, M. F. W. 2001. *Brief history of earth science education*. Blueprint for Change: Report from the National Conference, Earth and Space Science Education, June 21–24.

Lieberman, M. 1956. *Education as a profession*. Upper Saddle River, NJ: Prentice Hall.

Lortie, D. 1969. The partial professionalization of elementary teaching. In *The semi-professions and their organization: Teachers, nurses, social workers*, ed. A. Etzioni, 16–19. New York: Free Press.

National Education Association, Division of Field Service. 1968. Quoted in T. M. Stinnett, *Professional problems of teachers*, 54–55.

Sheppard, K., and D. M. Robbins. 2007. High school biology today: What the Committee of Ten actually said. *CBE Life Science Education* 6 (3): 198–202. Quoted in Science Education Wikipedia, 2008. *http://en.wikipedia.org/wiki/Science_education*

Stinnett, T. M. 1968. *Professional problems of teachers*. New York: Macmillan.

Tobias, S. 1997. *Faces of feminism: An activist's reflections on the women's movement*. Boulder, CO: Westview Press.

Chapter 4

The Long Shadow of No Child Left Behind:
Single-Faceted Accountability

Most teachers will do a good job without threats,
penalties, and rigid controls.

(Noddings 2007)

The January 2008 headline was ominous: "New York Measuring Teachers by Student Progress on Tests." And the story that followed was even more threatening to teachers' status, autonomy, and eventual job security.

The proposal, described as an "experiment," was to evaluate 2,500 New York City public school teachers on how much their students improve on annual standardized tests, providing data that would "eventually be used to help make decisions on teacher tenure or as a significant element in performance evaluations and bonuses." Ratings for individual teachers could even be made public (Medina 2008).

Thus comes full circle a movement begun in 2002 with the No Child Left Behind Act to assign responsibility to particular schools for students' failure to improve as measured by their performance on standardized tests of math and reading. According to NCLB rules, school districts are obliged to close entire schools that "fail" their students six years running. And, at least for a certain set of teachers in New York City and most likely Washington, D.C., it's now not just the schools, but also the teachers who are going to have to pay for students' poor test results, in lost earnings, status, and career prospects. Randi Weingarten, president of New York City's United Federation of Teachers, comments that, "If permitted, this would be one of the worst [policy] decisions of my professional life" (Medina 2008, p. 18).

This particular experiment was hastily aborted when in the spring of 2008, the New York legislature, lobbied by the teachers' unions and many others, passed state regulations prohibiting the use of student performance data in granting or withholding teacher tenure—at least for the immediate future (New York City Department of Education 2008).

But applying statistical measures of "teacher effectiveness" (called Value-Added Assessment Methodology, or VAM) is not going to go away. Powerful proponents of VAM are determined to perfect quantifiable measures no longer of teachers' generally defined "skills" in the classroom but of teacher productivity as measured by pupils' performance. The system, like NCLB itself, is openly modeled on that of the private sector. In the same way that "the labor market differentially rewards skills and productivity," says Dan Goldhaber of the Center on Reinventing Public Education at the University of Washington and a proponent of VAM, so must education free itself from a focus on teacher licensure and move toward quantitative assessment of teacher effectiveness (2008).

Effectiveness becomes a quantitative entity measured by comparing anticipated pupil achievement in a particular subject in a particular year (given demographics, prior achievement, expectations) to actual achievements (measured only by test results) at the end of the year. The teacher is then judged by the "value added," or not added as the case may be.[1]

Some History

In 2001, speaking for the Bush administration, Rod Paige, former school superintendent in Houston, Texas, and then newly appointed U.S. secretary of education, began a multistate effort to push for "accountability" in the nation's locally controlled schools. This led to the No Child Left Behind Act, signed into law

---

1. More details on the methodology can be found by viewing all five PowerPoint presentations at the Value-Added Methodology Seminar; see Goldhaber (2008).

January 8, 2002. Using the corporate model (setting measurable results and assigning responsibility for achieving those results), the Bush administration determined that all U.S. students needed to achieve grade-level reading and math proficiency by 2014. The fact that measuring science proficiency was not in the mix, as we would hear from science teachers we interviewed, made it more difficult than before to get state departments of education, school boards, and school administrators to support the science curriculum. But math and reading had the Bush administration's attention. And so they set about designing a system that would be imposed on all school districts eligible for federal money to measure (and control) progress in meeting their goals.

Some will argue that the basis for NCLB predated Rod Paige; that it was laid in the 1990s "standards movement" that was meant to combine the positive aspects of centralized curriculum guidelines with the individuality and energy of the U.S. local-control system. Student performance accountability systems, rather than detailed regulations, would structure the priorities of schools and districts and press them to make the changes necessary to deliver effective teaching to all of their students" (Resnick, Stein, and Coon 2008, p. 103). Instead, the system was virtually "hijacked" by low-level skills testing and, as this chapter will attest, teachers—even those whose subjects were not immediately covered by NCLB—were left to deal with the fallout.

NCLB has a nice egalitarian ring to it. Who would countenance leaving any child "behind?" But the model is decidedly corporate. It was believed that the best way to handle student underachievement (think of unsatisfactory storewide sales) was to set schoolwide improvement standards, test students annually, and then punish schools (close the stores) that did not meet their goals.

The Results

In the years since NCLB went into effect, 4,500 schools nationwide serving more than two million children (or about 8% of all federally funded schools) have failed to bring enough students to grade level. Some of these schools have failed only two years in a row; some four years in a row. After six years of "failure," as defined by the act, a school faces "restructuring," which could involve handing over control to the state or to a private management company, bringing in an entirely new staff, hiring "turnaround specialists," or opening charter schools in place of the public school targeted for elimination.

In fact, the federal government has been slow to eliminate schools, but the threat is always there. And the specter of teacher salaries and bonuses being tied mainly to student achievement is also there. In 2005, Denver voters agreed to allocate $25 million a year to a plan that linked teachers' salaries (in the aggregate) to how 70,000 students in the district tested. (See the section on teacher pay in Chapter 5 [pp. 61–70] for more details about the Denver plan.) Most states have responded to the threat of school closings by lowering their standards (states have control over the design and content of the annual tests), a process that caused *U.S. News & World Report* to describe national standards as a "race to the bottom" (Ramirez 2007, p. 50).

The Future of NCLB

In November 2008, the United States elected a new president. Since NCLB originated with the outgoing president, and his handpicked secretary of education (Rod Paige, later replaced by Margaret Spellings), there is now a new secretary of education, committed to raising pupils' performance particularly in inner-city schools, but not (yet) a diehard supporter of NCLB in its present form. Thus, there will be an opportunity to eliminate or radically restructure the act. It is noteworthy that, even on George W. Bush's watch, the reauthorization of the federal law had already stalled, allowing the opposition to this particular law (and to federally mandated testing more generally) to expand (FairTest 2008).

Also of interest—even though the election is over—were the two candidates' views on NCLB. John McCain, the Republican candidate, remained supportive of NCLB's basic approach. According to The Wall Street Journal (Chaker and Chozick 2008), he favored No Child Left Behind because, "NCLB has succeeded in shining a spotlight on how effectively schools are teaching.... The threat of tough sanctions gives schools a big incentive to improve."

Barack Obama's position during the campaign was more nuanced. While he wanted very much to "close the achievement gap," he also talked openly about fixing the failures of NCLB. He stated in public meetings, "We can meet high standards without forcing teachers and students to spend most of the year preparing for a single high-stakes test" (Obama and Biden n.d.).

The Impact of NCLB on Teacher Autonomy and Control

At the time of this writing, science had not been folded into the NCLB testing regime. Still, there is no question that in six short years its "long shadow" has changed science teachers' work lives just as it has changed the culture of schools, public and charter alike. (Private schools are exempt because they don't receive federal funding.) Teachers tell us they have lost control over not just what they cover but also the "pacing of the curriculum." In the past, even where teachers did not by themselves control curricular content, they could adjust the rate and sequence of their coverage. Denying them this right makes them feel, in yet another way, that they are more like assembly-line workers than professionals.

Indeed, according to one critic, "No Child Left Behind does not trust teachers to teach and evaluate their students. Rather the NCLB accountability system substitutes technology (paper-and-pencil machine-scored tests) for teacher judgments on the matter of student progress" (Shannon 2004).

A whole set of other professionals make the determinations teachers used to make:

> States set goals and distribute those goals across grade levels. Educational scientists discover through experimentation the optimal route to meeting those goals. Educational businesses produce teacher-proof technology (textbooks with scripted teachers' manuals, work books, computer programs, tests) to map routes for teachers and students to follow. States compose tests that measure students' progress toward established goals. And federal officials provide financial incentives and penalties to states forcing them to employ their schemes. (Shannon 2004)

To summarize: To the extent that teachers' judgments are absent in the NCLB accountability system, teachers as evaluators are further devalued.

NCLB and the Secondary Science Teacher

On the one hand, in its first six years, the implementation of NCLB should not have bothered secondary science teachers—the subject and object of this book—because only pupils' progress in math and reading required testing. Science is supposed to come next, and in some school districts preparations are already underway. But in fact, NCLB has spawned a testing culture that has spilled over into annual yearly progress (AYP) requirements in all subjects, and a corporate community of psychometricians that knows how to lobby for its own continuance and expansion. That's why our website respondents (all teachers of secondary science), when asked how NCLB requirements have affected their work lives, have much to say.

Living within a testing culture, reports a science chair at a large urban high school in the Southwest, involves a spring semester calendar that looks like the one on page 50. (AIMS is the statewide variant on NCLB.)

Extracurricular Testing (AIMS = Arizona Instrument to Measure Standards)

Date	Test
February 26	AIMS Writing
February 27	AIMS Reading
March 3–14	Optional: Reading & Math Benchmark Assessment 9th–10th Grade
March 3–14	Writing Benchmark Assessment 9th–10th Grade
March 4	AIMS Writing Make-Up
March 5	AIMS Reading Make-Up
March 17–28	Data entry Writing Benchmark Assessment 9th–10th Grade
April 8	AIMS Math
April 8	Terra Nova 9th Grade
April 9	AIMS Science (Proposed)
April 15	AIMS Math Make-Up
April 16	AIMS Science Make-Up (Proposed)
April 18	TerraNova Make-Up Window Closes
April 28–May 9	Writing Benchmark Assessment 9th–10th Grade
May 5–12	Math & Reading Cumulative Benchmark Assessment 9th Grade
May 9–16	Writing Benchmark Data Entry 9th–10th Grade
May 12–6	Math & Reading Cumulative Assessment Data Entry 9th Grade

She describes the effects of this testing regimen on teachers and students in her school:

Even though the full student body is not involved in the testing, the school day is so thoroughly disrupted that many students simply take testing days off. Alternative activities such as an open gym and the showing of current movies are provided, but it is the unspoken assumption that students who are not required to test will stay home. Since the majority of the faculty is tied up in the testing process, it is inconvenient for the administration to accommodate the supervision of these students, let alone provide any genuine educational activities.

The district mandates quarterly writing assessments, previously for grades 9–12, this year, 9 and 10 only. These are administered in language arts classes, and the full faculty is responsible for the grading, which is accomplished during scheduled department meeting time, or on a Friday when teachers are expected to give up a planning period for this purpose. Faculty attendance is taken at these scoring sessions, which counts towards the recertification hours awarded at the end of the year for "professional development."[2]

---

2. Quoted with permission of the source.

The message of the many-layered, district-created assessments, the science chair concludes, is that teachers lack the skill or objectivity to evaluate their own students' learning, effectively discounting teachers' judgments. Worse yet, this one teacher predicts that the national climate of hyper-accountability that has spawned state exams, district benchmarks, common finals, and quarterly assessments will not raise either teacher performance or student achievement.

Research still confirms that the teacher—and the student's relationship with the teacher—are the most critical determinants in student performance. Some recent articles underscore how crucial it is for teachers to converse one-on-one with their students, especially as it affects literacy, writing, and language acquisition (Darling-Hammond 1999).

In a recent workshop for federal education policy makers, sponsored by the National Academy of Sciences, Drew Gitomar (Educational Testing Service) countered the prevailing message of the event when he noted that federally mandated education accountability systems were psychometrically weak, and predicated on mistrust between the actors and the system. "We spend too much time," he said, "on outcomes, and not enough time on process, or collective human judgment." He was shaking his head when he concluded that we had no idea what it means, really, for a child to be "proficient" in one subject or another (Flanagan 2008).

What Science Teachers Say About NCLB

In March 2008, we posted on our website these questions:

- How has NCLB, which focuses on reading and math, affected your teaching of science?

- How has NCLB affected your work life, your professional status?

Stewart, a chemistry teacher, writes,

> Schools in Delaware are judged to meet DSTP tests which measure pupils' "annual yearly progress" (AYP) based on reading, writing, and mathematics tests. Science is tested, but does not count toward AYP. Thus, we have fewer science teachers (and far less science taught) because we need more math and English teachers. As a result, chemistry classes now average over 30 students at all levels, including those with special needs. The schedule has been changed so that our laboratory courses average 33 percent less contact time with students.

A physics teacher from a large public school in Texas notes,

> I don't know how much NCLB has affected my teaching directly, even though I am sure it has somehow. I do know that NCLB seems to have slowed the progress of the gifted kids.

Another Texas teacher, who is responsible for AP chemistry and physics, tells how NCLB chased him from public schools:

> Five years ago, I was department chair and teaching AP chemistry and AP physics in a large public school. The school's new principal repeatedly reprimanded me for not doing the standards test preparation with these AP students…. Before the end of that school year, my teaching assignment had been changed to physical science and I knew that I was no longer welcome at that school.

Writes a teacher from Tennessee,

> As a physics teacher, I have always had the luxury of having only to teach students who elect to take my course. My average class size used to be 20 to 24 per class before NCLB. Now I have 28 to 30 so that other NCLB tested classes (physics is not tested) can have a smaller class size for better results. This forces me to work with students in physics who are not ready for my course.

Returning to the science chair from the southwestern high school:

> Effective teachers are already in touch with their students' progress and use it to inform their instruction. Those who lack this insight will gain it from mentoring and collaboration sooner than from a printout of test scores. This pseudo-accountability has become a game of juggling numbers to make it look like the gap is closing.

Taking Back Control of Accountability

Our view is this: Teachers have the will and the capacity to create their own systems of accountability. Despite reports to the contrary, teachers are in favor of multifaceted assessments of teachers' competence. Albert Shanker, founder of the American Federation of Teachers (AFT), urged teachers in 1985 to set and enforce their own standards:

> We don't have the right to be called professionals—and we will never convince the public that we are—unless we are prepared to decide what constitutes competence in our profession and what constitutes incompetence and apply those definitions to ourselves and our colleagues. (Toch and Rothman 2008, p. 15)

Despite Shanker's admonition, the teachers' unions have tended to allow others to define and enforce school accountability. What they strongly oppose, as do the teachers we met researching this book, is the exclusive use of test scores for accountability and, in particular, the type of tests for measuring achievement in the sciences, when inquiry-based learning is precisely what is called for.

Science education activists, such as Richard Hake in physics, are alarmed at the type of testing NCLB is likely to use to measure science achievement. He fears that the way the tests are likely to be constructed will promote "direct instruction" (the old-fashioned kind of science teaching) instead of "interactive engagement" or "guided inquiry," which is what's called for in the national standards (NRC 1996; Hake 2005).

Contrary to NCLB proponents who would have us believe that teachers are opposed to any and all measures of accountability, there are other methods, endorsed by teachers, already in use that measure secondary science students' progress:

- Some states are already using work samples and performance-based assessments that, though more expensive than multiple-choice tests, measure inquiry-based science skills.

- The College Work and Readiness Assessment (CWRA) presents students with a single 90-minute problem in which they are asked to solve a pollution crisis, or deal with the influx of immigrant patients at a health clinic. Pupils being tested are allowed to use online newspaper editorials and research reports and then frame their own solution in writing.

The United Kingdom which, too, has national standards in science, has developed a national assessment designed to measure students' ability, given a toolkit of applications, to "finding things out," "developing ideas," and "exchanging and sharing information." What is of particular interest to us is that in the grading of these tests, student actions are tracked and mapped against expected abilities for that level of education. Thus, the U.K.'s test results provide both national scores and detailed feedback teachers can use productively (Silva 2008).

Even if more sophisticated student assessments were to be selected, U.S. science teachers do not want any single test of student achievement to be the means of holding schools and teachers accountable. They are not alone in this view. In 2005, the National Research Council, which represents the research arm of the National Academies of Science (and not the Department of Education) assigned a Committee on Test Design for K–12 Science Achievement to help states prepare for the implementation of NCLB—when and if it includes science. The Committee concluded, "A single assessment strategy cannot provide all of the information that education decision makers need to support student learning" (Committee on Test Design for K–12 Science Achievement 2005, p. 5).

So why did the science community go along with NCLB? One answer is provided by then-executive director of the National Science Teachers Association Gerald Wheeler (who also wrote the foreword to this book):

> We wrestled with this quite a bit in the formation of NCLB. We didn't want to be part of the testing process because we knew the assessments would not be aligned with our goals. Yet, we felt pretty strongly that if science weren't there, it would slide right off the school curriculum.[3]

There you have it. Play ball or risk losing science altogether.

Measuring Classroom Practice: Alternatives to NCLB

Seeking out other means of assessing teacher quality, we went back to the period just before the introduction of No Child Left Behind to find measures of teacher effectiveness that were already in operation or being recommended. In 2000, two years prior to the NCLB Act, the Educational Testing Service (which administers the SAT and other nationwide tests), published a report by Harold Wenglinsky that reminded those who would judge teachers, either by their prior preparation or by student performance, that "classroom practice" is at least as important—most particularly in the teaching of mathematics and science. And, even more relevant for the argument we are developing in this chapter, Wenglinsky (2000) provided evidence that classroom practice (such as the teaching of higher-order thinking skills and hands-on laboratory skills) can be accurately assessed by direct observation.

Some years later, after No Child Left Behind was changing the landscape by focusing teacher evaluation exclusively on high-stakes testing of pupils, Educational Testing Service returned to the theme in 2004, posting an issue paper provocatively titled *Where We Stand on Teacher Quality* (ETS 2004). Echoing its earlier position, the newer document called for—in addition

---

3. Gerald Wheeler, personal communication to the authors.

to other measures of teacher quality—"an ongoing series of rigorous, uniform, performance assessments" to be administered to veteran teachers by "trained reviewers following a standard observation protocol." To be sure, such assessments would be used "in concert with student achievement data as indicators of teacher quality," that is, not used alone (ETS 2004, p. 3). But it is interesting that direct observation is still seen by the largest student-testing agency in the country to be reliable.

What can we conclude from these documents? Let ETS speak for itself: "ETS believes strongly that the teaching skills and content knowledge of teachers [can and] should be routinely observed in the classroom and evaluated throughout their careers" (ETS 2004, p. 10).

Direct Observation: ETS's Praxis III

Why was ETS so confident that teaching skills and content knowledge could be evaluated by classroom observation? The reason is that it had developed a workable model, called Praxis, in the 1990s that is still in use in selective locations.

Praxis involves a three-pronged teacher licensure exam consisting of Praxis I, a basic reading and math test; Praxis II, a series of subject-matter tests; and Praxis III (most pertinent to our discussion here), a performance assessment specifically to evaluate a new teacher's classroom practice (Dwyer 1994).

After the Praxis III project was finished, Charlotte Danielson, a member of the ETS team, realized that the Praxis model need not be limited to the assessment of new teachers but could be used to support teachers at every level. She thereupon applied what she had learned at ETS to create a "framework for teaching" that makes it possible to do an assessment by direct observation of classroom teaching and teacher artifacts. This would permit, Danielson argued, a way to measure a teacher's

- planning and preparation,
- classroom environment,
- instruction, and
- professional responsibilities.

The system is incorporated in her books *Teacher Evaluation to Enhance Professional Practice* (with McGreal, 2000) and *Enhancing Professional Practice: A Framework for Teaching* (2007).

That framework, just as ETS's original Praxis III model, relies on trained observers, which is what bumps up the cost of direct observation. So much so, that only two states (at the present writing), Ohio and Arkansas, use Praxis III statewide in teacher licensing.

But, we will argue, the approach is worth wider adoption, if not at the state level then at the local level, because (even including the cost of training observers) it will serve as a measure equal to or more valid than student test scores.

California's PACT

Another newer teacher accountability model to watch is the Performance Assessment for California Teachers (PACT) that examines how teachers plan, teach, and evaluate student learning in the classroom. Developed by a consortium of 30 teacher-education programs in the state, PACT was initially designed to make certain that all candidates for the California teaching credential meet a uniform set of standards. Since summer 2008, candidates in all California teacher-education programs are expected to put together extensive portfolios drawn from their student teaching or internship experience similar to those required of teachers applying for National Board Certification. Both models are rooted in Danielson's work.

Teacher Advancement Program (TAP)

Meanwhile, a national Teacher Advancement Program (TAP) now in 200 schools gives experienced teachers the opportunity to advance professionally and to earn higher salaries by means of direct observation. Managed by the National Institute for Excellence in Teaching, the Teacher Advancement Program encourages teachers to move up in rank from career teacher to mentor teacher to master teacher. In each instance, teachers are evaluated on their performance in the classroom by Danielson-like rubrics as well as their students' test scores. (TAP is also being used to reward teachers who teach hard-to-staff subjects like science and math as well as those who teach in hard-to-staff schools.) What's also unusual about TAP is that teachers in a particular school must vote to join the program, which places them in charge (instead of simply at the receiving end) of the system's adoption.

The Classroom Observation and Analytic Protocol

Specifically for science teachers, there is the Classroom Observation and Analytic Protocol, developed by Horizon Research in North Carolina, and funded by the National Science Foundation for wider adoption (see *www.Horizon-*

Research.com). A typical guide (for the North Cascades and Olympic Science Partnership) provides a checklist for evaluating not just the science content and instructional methods in a teacher's classroom, but the "classroom culture," that teacher engenders.

Whether the students in that science classroom "make sense of," "reflect on their own understanding" and "make connections with prior experiences in and out of school" are also operationalized in specific items on the protocol.

All the programs described in this section clearly benefit when teachers select standards and rubrics as well as conduct evaluations. Right now, the only teacher evaluations with consequences (apart from high-stakes testing of pupils' achievement) is conducted by principals. Teachers would like these evaluations to be done more consistently and to include performance criteria applied to principals, too. What stands in the way of teachers evaluating principals is that most state statutes and negotiated agreements make evaluative criteria a "management" prerogative.

Conclusion

Even though it was not part of the NCLB rollout, which focused on math and reading, science has not been entirely exempt from high stakes testing. Many states already include science in their statewide assessments of pupils' achievement. But the consequences of using a series of science tests for making important decisions about students, teachers, and administrators, and for evaluating individual schools and school systems, could be dire (Nichols and Berliner 2008).

Secondary science teachers are nervous, and not just because—as has been the case with the testing of math and reading—their standing, their value to their schools, and maybe even their salaries and tenure will become linked to their pupils' achievement on these tests. They are also nervous because science is not like math and reading. It is both more than and less than a set of learned skills. Science depends on reading skills and calculation. But it is so much broader. It is a content subject. But it is also a process subject. The "problems" an able science teacher presents his or her students are not like math problems yielding to a single right answer, but more like puzzles inviting discussion and dissent. Above all, and students need to learn this early, science knowledge is made up of both knowns and not-yet-knowns, certainties, and disputes. Here's one description of the tasks of a science unit (involving a fieldwork study) as described by an observer:

The students in the two classes had many opportunities to reflect on their increasing knowledge as well as on the puzzles they encountered. In explaining why the trees on one side of the yard were taller, the students were aware of the limitations of their evidence with respect to the age of the trees. When reporting on their findings after a fieldwork activity, they asked each other questions about the quality and reliability of the data they were collecting. Increasingly, they asked for evidence from one another when causal explanations were proposed. (Michael, Shouse, and Schweingruber 2008, p. 30)

This set of activities falls in a quadrant of science instruction called "reflecting on scientific knowledge." But there are other elements that the science teacher is obliged to cover: "Understanding scientific explanations," "generating scientific evidence," "participating in science" by way of field trips (as described previously), laboratory work, or even discussion of current research in science—are all part of the science curriculum. The science teacher's responsibility is not only to convey these facts and insights but also to make the "ah-ha" reaction happen in his or her classroom; above all, to structure tests as a way of underscoring how varied the routes to scientific understanding can be.

Every science teacher interviewed for this book knows and tries to do all this. But as their range of instruction narrows (and with high-stakes testing it will narrow still more), science teachers may be forced to sacrifice everything they and their students love about science for a regimen of drill-and-practice. Their responsibility to their schools and their school districts will demand that.

But what of their responsibility to the nation's desperate need to replenish its science workforce? And to the next generation of science teachers? And to their own professional integrity? Who will be watching out for these?

References

Chaker, A. M., and A. Chozick. *Wall Street Journal*. 2008. Candidates Split Sharply on Bush's No Child Left Behind Law. May 29.

Committee on Test Design for K–12 Science Achievement. 2005. *Systems for state science assesssment*. Washington, DC: National Academies Press.

Danielson, C. 2007. *Enhancing professional practice: A framework for teaching*. 2nd ed. Alexandria, VA: Association for Supervision and Curriculum Development.

Danielson, C., and T. L. McGreal. 2000. *Teacher evaluation to enhance professional practice*. Alexandria, VA: Association for Supervision and Curriculum Development.

Darling-Hammond, L. 1999. *Teacher quality and student achievement: Review of state policy evidence*. Teaching Quality Policy Briefs No. 2. Seattle: University of Washington, Center for the Study of Teaching and Policy.

Dwyer, C. A. 1994. *Development of the knowledge base for the Praxis III: Classroom performance assessments assessment criteria.* Princeton, NJ: Educational Testing Service.

Educational Testing Service (ETS). 2004. *Where we stand on teacher quality.* Princeton, NJ: Educational Testing Service.

FairTest. 2008. What the presidential candidates are saying about NCLB. *www.fairtest.org/what-presidential-candidates-are-saying-about-nclb.*

Flanagan, N. 2008. In Einstein's lap. *Teacher Magazine* (January 9). Also available online at *www.edweek.org*

Goldhaber, D. 2008. Presentation at the Value-Added Assessment Methodology Seminar, Sacramento, California. October 6. *www.ctc.ca.gov/seminars/seminars-VAM.html*

Hake, R. R. 2005. Will the NCLB Act promote direct instruction of science? *Bulletin of American Physical Society* 50 (1): 851.

Medina, J. *New York Times.* 2008. New York Measuring Teachers by Test Scores. January 21.

Michael, S., A. W. Shouse, and H. A. Schweingruber. 2008. *Ready, set, science! Putting research to work in K–8 science classrooms.* Washington, DC: National Academies Press.

National Research Council (NRC). 1996. *National science education standards.* Washington, DC: National Academy Press.

New York City Department of Education. 2008. Directive, chancellor's office, June 1.

Nichols, S. L., and D. C. Berliner. 2008. *Collateral damage: How high-stakes testing corrupts America's schools.* Cambridge, MA: Harvard Education Press.

Noddings, N. 2007. Foreword. In *Collateral damage: How high-stakes testing corrupts America's schools,* ed. S. L. Nichols and D. C. Berliner, xiv. Cambridge, MA: Harvard Education Press.

Obama, B., and J. Biden. n.d. Barack Obama and Joe Biden's plan for lifetime success through education. *www.barackobama.com/pdf/issues/PreK-12EducationFactSheet.pdf.*

Ramirez, E. 2007. One standard fits all. *U.S. News & World Report* (November 2). Also available online at *www.usnews.com/education/articles/2007/11/02/national-standards.html*

Resnick, L. B., M. K. Stein, and S. Coon. 2008. Standards-based reform: A powerful idea unmoored. In *Improving on No Child Left Behind: Getting education reform back on track,* ed. R. D. Kahlenberg, 103. Washington, DC: Century Foundation Press.

Shannon, P. 2004. The faulty logic of NCLB. In *Saving our schools: The case for public education, saying no to "No Child Left Behind,"* ed. K. Goodman, P. Shannon, Y. Goodman, and R. Rappoport, 27–32. Berkeley, CA: RDR Books.

Silva, E. 2008. Measuring skills for the 21st century. *Education Sector Reports* (November 10).

Toch, T., and R. Rothman. 2008. Rush to judgment: Teacher evaluation in public education. *Education Sector Reports* (January 29).

Wenglinsky, H. 2000. *How teaching matters: Bringing the classroom back into discussions of teacher quality.* Princeton, NJ: Educational Testing Service, Policy Information Center.

Chapter 5

The Essentials Under Siege

Most teachers will do a good job without threats,
penalties and rigid controls.

(Noddings 2007)

This chapter deals with what the United States has long believed are the essentials with regard to teacher compensation: pay, tenure, and the presence or absence of unions in determining teachers' compensation and working conditions. The chapter also includes some recent efforts to effect change, not because they are widespread but because they are interesting and might herald a trend. But what our respondents have communicated to us over the two years we have been listening to them is that what is essential may not be sufficient to build a steady and renewable supply of secondary science teachers, most particularly as Generation Y makes its way into the workforce. And so we have to go beyond the essentials. But first, the essentials.

Part I: Teacher Pay

How much of a deterrent is teacher pay? How much of a difference does compensation make in recruitment and retention, most particularly of secondary science teachers? Would pay differentials by subject taught increase the appeal of science teaching? Or would it take an overall doubling of teacher pay?[1]

---

1. Many surveys are finding that working conditions might actually trump pay, but pay remains a factor. See *www.edweek.org/ew/articles/2008/01/10/18conditions.h27.html*.

The average salary for beginning teachers holding master's degrees in the United States is $38,500 for a 40-week contract, with a range of $29,000 (Alabama) to $47,000 (Manhattan). Twenty years later given annual increments, that Alabama teacher will be earning $42,000, the teacher in Manhattan $67,000.

Compare this (as beginning teachers will do) to the starting salary for bachelor's degree holders in the private sector who major in science and engineering. Gerald Wheeler, executive director emeritus of the National Science Teachers Association, observes that a student with a degree in science or engineering can land a job in a science-related industry with a starting salary 50% higher than that of a science teacher and expect regular annual increases (Wheeler 2008).

Recent economic downturns have resulted in some slowing of teacher attrition. Many teachers have been forced to postpone their retirement plans after seeing their nest eggs shrivel. States are reporting an overall easing in teacher shortages for the first time in years. School district officials credit the worsening economy and the growing population of unemployed white-collar workers lining up for teaching jobs with providing a temporary solution to their staffing problems. But, despite the growth of the applicant pool, there still remain critical shortages in hard-to-staff subjects like math and science (Stewart 2009).

To be sure, a 40-week school year (compared with a 50-week year in other jobs) is a positive factor for some workers, most especially parents who like being on the same school schedule as their children. But young people, competing with their peers on measures of earnings and status, pay close attention to starting salary and are put off both by the amount of pay and by the fact that salary increases for teachers are not normally based on merit, but on postgraduate credits and years of service.

Erik Brogt, a Dutch scholar studying U.S. science education, finds any shortfall of secondary science teachers baffling: Given the laws of supply and demand one would expect science teacher compensation would increase.[2] This does not seem to be the case, and the reasons are interesting: For one, it is not customary to pay teachers in one subject more than teachers in another subject. Where such rules pertain, the pay problem is "solved" by redefining teachers' specialties.

Simply put, a state having a shortage of secondary science teachers will opt to have more science subjects covered by nonspecialists and/or rely heav-

---

2. Erik Brogt, personal communication, unpublished paper.

ily on alternate routes to certification. That will ensure that every classroom is covered but by fewer specialists in physical science, Earth science, biology, and chemistry teaching those subjects (Hudson 1986).

What about other pay-related incentives? Hiring bonuses? Pay for performance? Paid summer internships in industry, universities, and government labs built in to teacher contracts? Retiring (or eliminating the need entirely for) student loans? Some school districts provide housing allowances if teachers will live near their schools. But do these incentives work?

Financial incentives such as forgivable loans are becoming a favored mode of federal and state support for teachers willing and able to teach math and science. Many of these scholarship opportunities are not promoted as well as they might be, but that will come. California is the exception. There, posters that promise free tuition for teachers invite undergraduates to apply for Noyce scholarships on every CSU campus.[3]

Some school districts are trying to lure new math and science teachers with signing bonuses of up to $10,000. New York City, having the nation's largest school district, recently targeted science and math teachers with special housing incentives that included $5,000 for a down payment (Dillon 2007b).

The Principle of Equivalency

Underlying a downward trend in science teachers' pay is the *principle of equivalency*—as we are calling it—based on a widely held view that teaching a subject, any subject, to a class of learners, of any age, at any stage, is equivalent work, requiring equivalent (if not identical) training, and of equivalent value to the school, the school district and the state. Thus, it is possible for a school district in the United States to designate equivalent starting salaries for a new teacher of physics and a new teacher of kindergarten, as long as their degree levels (bachelor's, bachelor's plus 12, master's, master's plus 12) are the same. They are further homogenized, one might say, by having their respective salaries increase by the same increment entirely by year of service.

Unions are said to play a large part in mandating "equivalence" in teacher contracts. The reason for this is most likely that, given the ratio of elementary to secondary teachers in the nation (3 to 1), by far the bulk of union mem-

---

3. Scholarship programs for prospective science and math teachers are available including:
    1. Noyce Scholarship (National Science Foundation): $10,000 per year for two years' college work in preparation for science/math teaching.
    2. Teacher Loan Forgiveness (Department of Education): $17,500 loan repayment.
    3. Perkins Loans: Teachers of math and science can have up to 100% of loan cancelled.
    4. Transition to Teaching: Provides funds to school districts and colleges to pay financial incentives of up to $5,000 to other professionals interested in teaching in high-needs schools.

bers are, most likely, elementary/middle school teachers themselves. But the salary ladder is part of a tradition in public education in which schools rely on credentials to set pay levels rather than teacher performance, however that is measured. Critics of the traditional framework say, "Paying teachers with the same credentials—and the same number of years of experience— exactly the same salaries devalues their uniqueness and the importance of their being effective in the classrooms" (Toch and Rothman 2008).

Given recent shortages, some school districts have sought means of sidestepping the rules: providing "incentives" in the way of higher salaries (and "off scale" start-up packages) for new teachers. We think it's significant that, in 2008, for the first time, the National Science Teachers Association (NSTA) openly encouraged states, districts, and schools to explore differential pay systems that would encourage "more qualified individuals to enter the science education profession.

Pay for performance and merit pay (see below for the distinction between the two) have not been an easy sell. Nor do union contracts encourage differentiation on any other basis but degree attainment and years on the job. So, until the changes recommended by NSTA are implemented nationwide, secondary science teachers are stuck with equivalency.

Science teachers wishing to increase their take-home pay have few options within teaching: becoming a science chair is one; teaching summer school is another. But for a significant raise, a teacher has no option but to get certification in education administration and become a principal.

Pay for Performance

"Long Reviled, Merit Pay Gains Among Teachers," ran a *New York Times* headline in June 2007. Starting with certain districts, state and federal money is making it possible for school districts to offer merit pay as part of "teacher professionalization"[4] (Dillon 2007a, p. 1). The additional money is coming from the U.S. Department of Education's Teacher Incentive Fund, launched in 2006, which has so far awarded $80 million to states for such merit pay.

On what basis is "merit" to be assessed? On this there is little agreement because the law requires only that districts use "objective measures" of student performance as *part* (italics ours) of the award criteria. Details are left up to the locals and there are as of this reckoning, 34 models in play (Sawchuck 2009). Thus, while the merit pay advocates within the federal government (in accordance with No Child Left Behind) want teacher performance tied directly to pupils' performance in a single year, South Carolina mixes student

---

4. The awards range from a few hundred dollars to $10,000.

achievement (30%) with classroom observation (40%). Others want school-wide student achievement added to the mix to reward teacher collaboration. Critics point out that the jury is still out as to the effectiveness of teacher pay-for-performance programs. But, as Matthew Springer, director of the National Center on Performance Incentives at Vanderbilt University, readily concedes, that's because there is very little rigorous research on the program's impact on schools (Springer 2009).

Even with the allowance for local control, certain state unions are balking at that single criterion even as they and some teachers embrace (for the first time) the principle of merit pay.

Although "merit pay" and "pay for performance" are often used interchangeably, a Citizens' Commission on Civil Rights document offers the following distinction:

- *Performance pay* is linked to student achievement.

- *Merit pay* is a broader concept that rewards teachers for a variety of improvements. (Taylor and Rosario 2007, p. 4)

Other means of delivering differential pay, such as signing bonuses and higher pay for work in high-needs schools, are also on the table, as are issues such as the "bumping rights" of senior over junior teachers (a privilege of teacher seniority). But so far only the Denver School Board (see the next section) has successfully negotiated a merit pay system.

One way to provide career advancement for teachers—independent of merit or performance pay—is to schedule growth steps, such as has been done in the Rochester, New York, school district over the past 20 years, but is not yet more widely adopted. Rochester teachers enjoy four career development stages: intern, resident, professional, and lead teacher, with progress from one to the other depending on peer review. Normally, the intern stage takes up the entire first year for new teachers; teachers are placed in the resident stage for an additional four years, during which time they are expected to earn certification, a master's degree, and tenure. After achieving these goals, teachers attain the status of "professional teacher" where most remain for the duration of their career. Ten percent go on to serve as mentors and curriculum development specialists, that is, "lead teachers."

Denver's Merit Pay Experiment: ProComp

In 2005, voters in Denver, Colorado, approved a $25 million tax increase to fund a new nine-year merit-based pay system for the city's teachers. Pro-Comp, as the system is called, was intended to be an alternative to Denver's (typical) lock-step salary schedule for teachers, based on years of service and higher education coursework. As reported by *The Denver Post*, ProComp will tie raises or bonuses for teachers to some or all of the following special conditions:

- Positive professional evaluations
- Setting and then meeting objectives for improving student learning
- Working in hard-to-staff (usually inner-city) schools
- Working in hard-to-staff subjects (such as science)
- Building (new) professionally relevant skills

Note what's missing: the darling of No Child Left Behind, namely tying teachers' raises to pupils' numerical gains on standardized tests.

The effect of a ProComp merit pay increase could be substantial. Teachers with a master's degree and 60 units beyond a bachelor's degree would normally see their salary stall at about $68,000, plus modest cost-of-living adjustments for the last half of their career. Under ProComp, such teachers can keep earning raises until retirement, effectively putting their career-end salary as high as $90,000.

What is making the initiative possible are both the Denver teachers union's willingness to incorporate ProComp into teachers' contracts and Denver voters' willingness to tax themselves for a better pay plan for their teachers in hopes of a better education for their children.

Brad Jupp, the chief union negotiator (himself a teacher), told a *Denver Post* reporter why pay for performance is so difficult to implement in general and why it took so long for Denver teachers to move on the issue. Public schools have a harder time making changes, especially in the way people are paid:

> First, we don't have a history of measuring results and we don't have a results-oriented attitude in our industry [unlike the private sector with its bottom line].... Furthermore we have configured the debate so that it's a conflict between heavyweight policy contenders like unions and school boards. Finally, we don't have direct control over our revenue. It's easier to change a pay system when there is a rapid change in revenue that can be oriented to new outcomes [again, in contrast to the private sector]. Most school finance systems provide nothing but routine cost of living adjustments. (Mead 2006)

What made the reform possible in Denver, Jupp asserts, was the complete cooperation of the teachers' union. Jupp himself was the chief union negotiator with the school board and was and remains an enthusiast for Pro-Comp. And what makes the new system particularly remarkable is that it managed to satisfy those who simply want higher pay for teachers and those who want to see increased pay tied to very specific outcomes (Moulthrop, Calegari, and Eggers 2006).

Much has already been learned in the Denver experiment. For one, differentiated pay does not destroy workplace morale. For another, a $1,000 bonus will not be enough to persuade a teacher to leave a middle-class school for an inner-city school. But $1,000 per year can motivate a teacher in a high-poverty school to stay there.

The question is, Will any other states or school districts follow Denver's lead?

What Science Teachers Say About Salary

Teacher interviewees and respondents (admittedly self-selected) to our questions about salary posted on our website were divided about which variables ought to enter into the pay equation. Respondents explored several issues related to secondary science teachers' salaries.

First, many suggested that teacher salaries are not the key issue. For these respondents, the intrinsic rewards of teaching are more important, as are autonomy, job security (see the next section on tenure), and the opportunity to be creative and pursue a calling. For them, these freedoms more than outweigh the disadvantages of lower-than-market-value salary.

Rob is a high-school science chair in one of the largest school districts in Oregon. He has a B.S. in mechanical engineering and worked for several years in fire protection. Both his parents are teachers (his father a physics teacher), and though Rob really enjoyed his engineering career, he was working very long hours that got in the way of starting a family. So he got his master's in teaching and went to one district for a year, then came to his current district, where he's been teaching for 14 years. He has taught freshman physical science, and physics, and is now part of a nationally recognized engineering program. He has also been the science department chair for the past six years.

Rob says that, unlike some of his colleagues, he knew, because of his parents, that teaching would not be easy. Not only does it require classroom management and interpersonal skills, but the teacher also must really understand how to relate to adolescents, not only how they learn. Furthermore, as others in this book have remarked, lab-based courses require a tremendous amount of management and time.

Rob didn't choose to teach for the money, he says. "I was making a lot more as an engineer." So he's not critical of his take-home pay. But he distances himself from what he calls the "union mentality":

The idea that all teachers are equal and that their pay should be based on years of experience and education level keeps schools from attracting and retaining instructors with technical expertise.... We should be willing to pay market value for teachers in high-need fields.

An important form of "compensation" for Rob, which became obvious as the interview progressed, was that teaching provided him with an opportunity to become a leader. Furthermore, he was able to introduce a new engineering-in-the-schools curriculum and to become and remain science department chair. That, too, is compensation for some.

Will is another émigré. He left research science for secondary science teaching. In Will's case, his compensation as an academic researcher was low because, without a PhD, he would inevitably hit a glass ceiling. Going for the PhD would have been costly in many respects, including time, he reasoned, and so he left for teaching. He now believes it will take him less time and less money to get to the $70,000 top teacher's salary (in his region) than it might have in full pursuit of the role of principal investigator for a major study—a position for which, as he puts it, "many compete and only a few achieve."

There are, however, many secondary science teachers for whom pay is simply insufficient to support a family. Nicole, who teaches in a Northwest suburb, has had to work all but one summer in nine years. Mike one-ups Nicole during their joint interview: "I've had one summer off in 18 years," he says, "If I didn't work in the summers, things would be very difficult for me and my family." So for some teachers, at least, pay is not sufficient to allow summers off.

The issue for policy makers, however, is not just whether higher salaries attract qualified science teachers, but whether the current pay scale will discourage science teachers from staying in the field.

Differential Pay for Science Teachers

Some of our respondents, prompted by our questions on the website about teacher pay, wrote to the issue of pay differential for secondary science. Some argue that secondary science teaching is more time-consuming, and some say, more demanding, with more responsibilities than teaching other high-school subjects. Many specifically mentioned the extra time and responsibility required to set up and tear down labs and to order inventory and maintain equipment—responsibilities teachers in other content areas do not have.

Writes a retired biology teacher from Arizona,

High-school science teachers should be paid more due to the increased amount of prep time involved in teaching science classes. Moreover, science teachers are responsible for the safety of their students in laboratory exercises that involve experiments that can be dangerous. Teachers of other disciplines have commented to me, after observing my classes, that they were amazed by all of the classroom interactions that I had to supervise and manage, in addition to the actual teaching of the subject.

And writes a chemistry teacher from Colorado, who went through alternative licensure,

The principle of equivalence was a shock. I honestly couldn't believe that I earned what a physical education teacher earns. We in science do so much more work.

Writes a biology teacher from West Virginia,

Our state requires "50 percent hands-on" [in science], which is more work for the teacher than simply grading worksheets or lecturing. A salary supplement like extra duty pay might be appropriate for science teachers. All of the teachers in my department come early and stay late. They put in many more hours than the coaches.

From a physics teacher from Virginia,

Typically, for every one-hour [lab or hands-on] activity for the student, there are at least two hours of prep/post time. I do not know of a science teacher who can perform his or her professional tasks and obligations within the contract hours paid for.

And of the special demands of learning science, writes another retired biology teacher from Arizona,

The knowledge base of science teachers is more demanding than that of many other disciplines. Since we teachers are discipline specific, we must be current in the latest information relevant to our subjects. This requires that we attend workshops, classes, and science conventions on a regular basis so that we can provide our students with information and techniques for labs that are relevant to their needs. Most of this schooling we pay for ourselves.

Not all teachers agree that science teaching should be better paid than other subjects. Writes a biology teacher from North Carolina,

I am not one penny more important than the English teacher or the band and choral directors. Yes, I have far more specific knowledge than teachers of lower grades, but my knowledge is narrow and I spend far less time in contact with my students.

Our teacher respondents were truly divided about whether the supply-and-demand argument alone should lead to matching teacher pay to market value. Some responded negatively to the question, seeing salary as a reflection of the value put on science teaching, rather than a market-driven function. Writes a physics teacher from New York,

> Differential pay for teachers presumes a market-driven education system as an effective means of improving education…. Can you truly say that the value of what physics teachers offer is greater, and more worthy, than the value of what English teachers offer? Are science and math more important than literacy and culture?

Others avoided the values issue altogether, but wanted it acknowledged, as one of our respondents put it, that in certain sections of the country, there are 1.5 to 2 times as many elementary certified teachers for each available job. In science and mathematics there are fewer qualified people than there are openings.

Conclusion

How would one determine appropriate pay differentials if a school district were to permit them? Our respondents offered a variety of suggestions. Most agreed there should be better benchmarks for establishing a pay scale, something that supersedes supply and demand. A Michigan-based chemistry and physics teacher provides us with one possible conclusion to the issue of pay:

> Somewhere along the line, I was told that being a teacher was one of the hardest jobs in the world to do well and one of the easiest jobs in the world to do poorly—and still get paid the same.

What this teacher is suggesting and what underscores the thesis of this book, is that any pay scale has to be evaluated as to the degree to which it promotes professionalism by rewarding not just time in the classroom but also the many facets of quality instruction. Or, as the president of the St. Paul Minnesota Federation of Teachers expressed it, in an *Education Week* "webinar,"

> How do we assume that every dollar spent [on performance pay] doesn't just improve the teacher's salary, but also improves our professional day, attracts and retains high-quality teachers, and makes teaching an enduring career rather than a starter profession? (Ricker 2009)

What About That Vaunted Long Summer Vacation?

During July 2008, we thought it was appropriate to ask our web respondents the following question: *What do you do during your summer break?* The responses we received further illustrate the utmost in professionalism demonstrated by science teachers.

A chemistry teacher from California described summer vacation as,

Comp time to make up for the 70-hour workweek I do for 10 months a year. Teaching is not an 8 a.m. to 3 p.m. job with summers off. I do not know how to do that and stay current, creative, and on top of the game.

A short list of things science teachers tell us they did on their summer vacations includes:

- Writing new curriculum or revamping old curriculum

- Teaching summer school

- Attending workshops to learn new teaching techniques or new technical skills

- Doing research at universities or national science laboratories

- Attending science conferences

- Preparing for the next year's classes

- Attending college classes

- Attending workshops to learn how to implement new teaching methods

- Inventorying, ordering, cleaning, and repairing lab equipment

Even with so much to do in preparation for the coming school year, low salaries force many teachers into taking summer jobs.

An AP biology teacher from California puts it simply: "Every summer I work because my family needs the money."

Another problem teachers face is that during the school year there is virtually no time for doctor and dentist appointments or home repairs. So many teachers use the summer, as one biology teacher explains it, "to catch up with life."

Part II: Tenure

In any discussion of teacher tenure, it is important to realize that there is no such thing as lifetime "tenure" in the public schools. What public school teachers normally receive after some years on probation is a presumption in their favor that they will be rehired for many subsequent one-year terms, unless cause for not hiring them can be demonstrated (National Commission on Teaching & America's Future 1996).

Tenure protection for teachers was born in the state of California in 1921, followed 16 years later by Michigan in 1937. The reason for it was obvious at the time: Principals were firing teachers arbitrarily because of favoritism. Tenure has often been criticized fairly or unfairly. But today it is more seriously under siege. If the teacher evaluations embedded in the No Child Left

Science Teaching as a Profession

Behind Act (see Chapter 4) are ever linked to tenure, tenure might shortly end or be amended to the point of no return.

Currently, in most states, teachers achieve tenure after five years of satisfactory employment (or four, if they come with prior experience). "Satisfactory performance" is normally determined by classroom observations conducted by the principal, a teacher's response to guidance and mentoring, his or her rate of "improvement" where improvement is deemed necessary, and other professional measures. In other words, a teacher is supposed to be "peer reviewed" along peer-determined standards similar to other professions. But the new national focus on pupils' achievement (left to the states to implement) threatens to replace the former standards and even teacher tenure itself.

The first stirrings are already being felt. In 2005 there was a ballot proposition, endorsed by California's governor, called "Put Kids First." Had it passed, Proposition 74 would have altered the current tenure law in California in two ways. First, it would have raised the amount of time, from two years to five years, new teachers would have to wait before they were covered by job protection rules. Second, it would have allowed the school district to dismiss employees after two consecutive "unsatisfactory" performance evaluations.

The reason teachers objected so strongly is that quite often new teachers need more time—especially in the absence of a mentoring program—to realize their potential as teachers.

What's New: Tying Student Performance to Tenure

In 2007 as No Child Left Behind was making its way through the reauthorization process in the U.S. Congress, the New York Legislature weighed in with a mandate for statewide minimum standards for teacher tenure (Saunders 2007). It is one thing to set new tenure standards for new teachers. But if (as may have been intended) the New York state mandate were to apply to all teachers, including those with tenure, it would have meant that student test scores would be used to determine teacher tenure, and possibly even tenured teachers' dismissals.

By spring 2008, the New York Legislature had to back down, actually voting to prohibit the use of student scores in tenure decisions. But the threat is ever on the horizon, especially in districts without as powerful a local teachers union as that in New York (Medina 2008).

The grounds for dismissal of a tenured teacher, according to most state laws, are specific and only apply to very dire situations. Typically, there has to be proof of physical or mental conditions that render the individual unable or unfit to associate with children; immoral conduct; incompetence (not specifically defined), inefficiency, or insubordination; excessive absences; conviction of a felony or crime of moral turpitude (Missouri State Teachers Association n.d.). Teacher "incompetence" is always a factor, but not normally linked to student performance, either by observation or by tests.

Teachers' concerns go beyond simple job security (though this cannot be ignored). Efforts to tie tenure to pupil performance threaten to take away the right of self-regulation that is so essential to any profession. This explains why teachers, individually, and through their unions and associations, are so protective of tenure. Here's the gist of their argument:

> Teachers don't want incompetents in their profession. Incompetents make the job harder for the good teachers, and diminish the stature of the profession. Tenure doesn't protect incompetent teachers—incompetent school boards and their managers do! (Patchogue-Medford Congress of Teachers n.d.)

Raising the Bar for Tenure

"We're not talking about doing away with tenure. What we're talking about is making tenure a serious hurdle," says Thomas Kane (2007), an economist working with the Project for Policy Innovation at Harvard and a strong proponent for alternate methods of certification, teacher evaluation, and tenure. The plan, outlined in a Brookings Institution report, is intended to make it "harder to promote least effective teachers to tenured positions." Kane and his colleagues want schools to "set a minimum tenure standard" and to deny tenure to teachers below that standard…" (Gordon, Kane, and Staiger 2006, p. 10) and not provide tenure automatically after three or five years.

The Kane plan, a performance-based option, challenges other traditions within teacher certification and evaluation. Barriers to entry would be lowered (to accommodate Teach for America participants, for example). No longer would teachers need a traditional teaching degree or certification. One point of entry would be the traditional one. But another route "would be provided to novice teachers who have only the undergraduate degree and subject knowledge to get hired" (Gordon, Kane, and Staiger 2006, p. 10). Once hired, teachers may have a trial period of a couple of years. If offered tenure, it has to be based on performance. And "performance" is to be assessed on multiple measures, pupils' achievement to be only one of them.

Kane is both an economist and an education policy analyst, and he brings quantitative analysis to the argument for making tenure more "earnable" than is currently the case. For example, he points out that fewer than

1% of public or private school teachers are laid off (presumably for cause) in their first two years, which even if the number is undercounted by a magnitude of 10, means most new teachers who come in fully credentialed are making it to tenure (Gordon, Kane, and Staiger 2006, p. 13).

Also, he is well aware that a single measure of "teacher effectiveness"—even student achievement—should not suffice. And so his plan calls for new systems for evaluating teacher performance, systems that would include but not be limited to student academic performance. Much of the responsibility for teacher evaluation would fall on principals (who could call on outside and inside evaluators). But Kane is adamant that measures such as licensure, teachers' test scores, or postgraduation credits not be used to measure "excellence."

Kane knows that a rigorous performance-based system has to be perceived as fair by teachers who must live with it, if it is to succeed and to replace semiautomatic tenure (Gordon, Kane, and Staiger 2006, p. 22). Thus his plan calls for public review and public oversight. But his most potent argument, if it proves to be the case, is that high-stakes performance evaluation will improve the standing of teaching as a profession:

> Adoption of our proposal would signal that long-term standing in the teaching profession depends on a more challenging achievement [than mere certification]—success in the classroom. Our proposal would also enable teachers who demonstrate excellence in the most challenging classrooms to earn higher pay. That higher pay could also be coupled with other steps to elevate such high-performing teachers, such as use of master-teacher status.

The bottom-line issue is whether teachers and teacher unions will agree.

Why the Opposition to Teacher Tenure?

Teachers are not alone in expecting tenure after four or five years' probation. Workers in many other fields receive protection from unfair dismissal either through union contract or under civil service law. Teachers' professional work being as public as it is—and their standing in the classroom and the community being as exposed—means that more than many other professionals, teachers need and deserve protection. School boards are elected bodies which might, if they could, fire teachers whose political views they dislike. Finally, and most important, tenure protects teachers' academic freedom. See the recent efforts by the school boards in Topeka, Kansas, and in Dover, Pennsylvania, which succeeded in firing teachers who insisted on teaching Darwinian evolution—until the respective school boards themselves were recalled (Goldberg 2005; Leshner 2008).

Why, then, is there opposition to teacher tenure? The unions, which favor it, complain that school boards want to cut costs by substituting young, inexperienced teachers for those who are older and better paid. So long as tenure is in place, they can't. Some who oppose tenure argue that firing teachers can sometimes cost a school district as much as $200,000 in legal fees because of the constraints of tenure, serving to keep incompetent teachers in place (Small Newspaper Group 2005).

But there's another argument, brought forth by Thomas Kane, who, having found ways (to his satisfaction) to measure teacher effectiveness in grades 4–8, concludes that performance on the job rather than prehire criteria should be used as the basis for long-term teacher selection. Kane criticizes the current tenure system because it rewards "longevity rather than results" (Pettus 2006).

Swapping Tenure for Higher Pay

Another headline, another trend? Members of the Washington, D.C., Teachers Union, at all grades, in all subject areas, were scheduled to vote in September 2008 as to whether they would be willing to swap tenure for substantial increases in pay. Some, depending on field and training, would be able to earn as much as $131,000 after 14 years of teaching; the highest teacher salary at present is $87,000 in the District of Columbia. Along with performance-based pay and tenure changes, the cost of the new contract would be to dismantle the district's seniority system and teachers' guarantee of another classroom if their own school were reduced in size or closed (Sawchuk 2008).[5]

What else do we know about teachers' willingness to swap tenure for increased pay? In a wide-ranging survey of 1,010 K–12 public school teachers, researchers Ann Duffet, Steve Farkas, Andrew Rotherman, and Elena Silva in 2007 found a sizable majority not willing to give up tenure for higher pay. We found a much wider range of opinion when we asked the same question of the secondary science teachers who frequent our website.

We posted a three-part question to our web respondents in the spring of 2008: If you had the choice, would you trade tenure for a $5,000 pay increase? Trade tenure if the pay increase were a lot higher? Or, rather hold on to tenure?

A Michigan science teacher who got a negative performance review from the administration of her school, despite the fact that her students did

---

5. The vote, as of this writing, never took place. But nonetheless, the district is firing some and upgrading other teachers anyway. Teachers are skeptical.

10–12% better than others on the final exam, writes, "I've taught with and without tenure. If you have a supportive, nurturing administration, then tenure is completely unnecessary."

A New York state physics teacher makes two points. First, the tenure system causes new teachers to stay in one school environment instead of gaining more varied experience in other schools. Second, for himself personally, "Tenure has little value. As a physics teacher I satisfy a niche that is hard to fill."

A Virginia science teacher working in a private school feels differently about tenure. She writes,

> Tenure would be such a happy thought. I teach in a private school and we have one-year contracts for all. Often when teachers are let go, they are asked to give their lesson plans to the new teacher. If they were that good, why were they let go, one wonders.

A science teacher from California writes,

> Tenure is unnecessary until you need it! It is certainly not worth giving up for $5,000. I like tenure because it provides a system of checks and balances between administrators and teachers.

A physics teacher from Texas wonders what might take the place of tenure:

> Many of us teachers never grow beyond the first few years and are doing the same job at year 30 that we did at year five. That's an argument against tenure. But as we move away from a tenure system we will likely move away from a system of pay based on years of service. What will take its place? Maybe pay for value added to the school.

A recently retired science teacher from Illinois sees both sides:

> I have seen both good and bad results of tenure. Most important is the language of the contract. On the one hand, you want to be evaluated fairly. On the other, you don't want only those to get tenure who are just like you.

Let's let a science teacher from California have the last word:

> Tenure allows teachers due process. Without tenure, teachers are easy targets for dismissal, from parents, administrators, or anyone else with a disagreement about content or pedagogy.

Part III: Unions

Union membership muddies the issue of teachers' professional status. On the one hand, teachers, all levels, all subjects, have professional responsibility for the pupils in their classrooms. But they are at the same time employees of a school, which in turn is part of a school district managed by a publicly funded bureaucracy.

That's why unionization gets mixed reviews by the public at large. The public expects teachers to be dedicated, ever at the ready, contributing toward and resting on the public trust. When teachers threaten to, or go out on, strike and children are locked out of school, parents and taxpayers feel betrayed.

Not surprisingly, unionization came late to the American teacher.[6] But today, despite the controversies, the majority of teachers in the United States, including those who work in publicly chartered and private schools, have the right to join a teachers' union, either the National Education Association (NEA) or the American Federation of Teachers (AFT). Exceptions are in right-to-work states where unions are prohibited. Where teachers' unions are allowed, other school employees (teachers' aides, maintenance workers, nurses, and even administrators) may affiliate. Sometimes membership is mandatory. Elsewhere, an agency fee is imposed on every working teacher, member or not, for payment of partial union dues. Most often where the union has a districtwide contract, union dues may be automatically deducted from the paycheck.

Many teachers aren't aware, until they change schools, that the degree to which the "representing organization" or union can bargain for wages and working conditions and process grievances is dependent both on the laws of each state and on the content of individual contracts. That's why teachers meeting teachers from different jurisdictions will have very different experiences of teachers' unions. (See the dialogue later in this chapter between Tom and Mary Anne as an example, p. 81.)

So deep-seated is the notion of teachers' exemption from "ordinary" employee/employer relations that when Albert Shanker, the legendary teachers' union leader, who died in 2007, began his career back in the 1960s, union membership among New York City's teachers was about 5% of their total number. This was not surprising because, at the time, the union couldn't deliver much. Collective bargaining was assumed to be illegal, because, as public employees, teachers couldn't go on strike (another assumption Shanker

---

6. And to police, fire, and other medical personnel apart from doctors.

successfully challenged). So teachers had nothing to threaten if bargaining didn't go their way. After Shanker led the first successful teachers' strike in New York City's history, membership in his AFT affiliate climbed in six short years (1962–1968) from 5% to 97% (Kahlenberg 2007b).

The AFT has always been a union first, a professional association second. Its origins in 1916 during a decade of brutal repression of unions in other industries is one reason; its affiliation with the CIO (Congress of Industrial Organizations), another. The other teachers' union is the NEA (yes, a union despite its name). The NEA began in 1857, much earlier than the AFT, as an "association of teachers" and, because schools were effectively segregated until the 1960s, its members helped organize a parallel Association of Colored Teachers in 1904. (The two organizations merged in 1966.)

The NEA has worked long and hard for teacher's rights and benefits. In 1912, the NEA won a half-century battle for state pensions for teachers (in place by 1945 in every state), and in 1954 moved teachers' professionalism forward by helping create the National Center for Accreditation of Teacher Education (NCATE) which succeeded in establishing uniform national standards for teacher training.

With its 2.1 million members, the NEA has always registered about twice the number of teachers as the AFT. Together, the two associations would wield enormous influence if they merged. Yet merger talks have not yet succeeded.

The Professionalism Agenda

Unions are not limited to wage-and-hour and benefits issues. Protecting seniority is their lifeblood. And so the subtle and not-so-subtle attacks on teacher tenure that have surfaced in our surveys bear directly on union protection of professionalism. Unions have also been involved with teachers' professional development issues directly, with some larger districts providing professional development in-house. And, in recent decades, unions have participated in the development of curriculum standards. Their most direct engagement resulted in a set of prescriptions introduced in the 1980s for which they are not usually given credit for being the first.

Focusing on the idea that a profession ensures the quality of the service it provides to the public by educating and policing itself, the unions called for

- strengthening teacher preparation programs in universities by requiring an academic subject major,

- establishing standards for a National Teaching License,

- setting up peer evaluation/reviews and peer mentoring programs for new teachers, and

- defining career ladders that include positions of "lead" or master teacher. (Casey 2007)

At least as important to teachers' professionalism are the unions' efforts to prevent what they call the "de-skilling" of teaching, which means opposing the certification of lesser-trained school personnel to take on instructional tasks.

Unions as Advocates for Public Education

As a union leader, particularly one who would draw picket lines around classrooms, Shanker was controversial. But as a defender of public education, he and his coequals in the NEA have usually been willing to embrace "reform" as inevitably good for teachers, because it was good for public education, even where teachers resisted it (Kahlenberg 2007a). He argued that teachers' unions would enhance and defend public education, not destroy it. As proof, he was opposed to privatization, vouchers in particular, but charter schools as well, anything that would drain money, students, and parental support from public education. (Today, the AFT and NEA are not so hostile to alternative schools. In fact, some unions sponsor charter schools themselves.)

Albert Shanker himself fought at least as hard to protect teacher tenure, and recently both the NEA and AFT have been actively working to reform the No Child Left Behind Act. On behalf of teachers who believe they are being written out of both curriculum design and the setting of pupils' achievement criteria under NCLB, several AFT and NEA affiliates are filing briefs versus the U.S. Secretary of Education, claiming NCLB "interferes with the states' right to set policies for education" (Connecticut State Association of Teachers 2006).

At least as significant has been the unions' commitment to another vision of school reform. In contrast to those who are pressing for merit pay, charter schools, and alternative teacher certification, teachers' unions want to "raise inner-city pupils' achievement by equalizing educational funding across school districts," in effect guaranteeing those children high-quality facilities and smaller class size (Los Angeles Times 2008). Nevertheless, teachers unions are frequently described as "opposed" to the reform agenda. A recent opinion piece that originated in the *San Diego Union-Tribune* but then circulated in other papers is typical. The writer describes the unions and the teachers they represent as "putting the interests of adults before those of children" and as entities "that instinctively resist change." More ominously, he concludes, "If Education Secretary-Designate Arne Duncan wants reform, he is going to have to stand up to organized labor in the form of teachers unions" (Navarrette 2008)

In the face of opinions like this, the unions are going to have to work more effectively to persuade policy makers and the general public that they and the teachers they represent are, and have to continue to be, part of the solution.

New Challenges

In 2002 as NCLB was being debated and implemented across the United States, teachers and their union representatives began to fear that teachers' contracts at "failing schools" would be nullified—even where the contracts had been the product of collective bargaining. That, according to press reports, was the view (perhaps even the intention) of then Secretary of Education Rod Paige, who was pressing hard for NCLB (Keller 2006). Paige was not alone in his view that teacher evaluation should be written out of union contracts. Then Governor Mitt Romney (later Republican candidate for president) proposed a bill to the Massachusetts Legislature in 2006 that would have done just that.

> The governor's bill seeks to upend the status quo in teacher pay and evaluation that has been written into collective bargaining agreements across the Commonwealth [of Massachusetts]...it would make teachers in all subjects eligible for a bonus upon receiving an exemplary evaluation. [Thus] the bill would remove teacher evaluation from the collective bargaining process and establish statewide criteria for assessing each teacher's "contribution to student learning." (Hess and West 2006a)

Today, as NCLB is heading for reauthorization, there are still educational researchers and consultants who believe raising pupils' achievement, especially in math, science, and in the inner-city schools, is best done by challenging teachers' contracts and seniority. Here's the argument as laid out by The Heritage Foundation, a Washington think tank that advises Republicans:

According to the report, school officials should pursue six types of changes in teachers' contracts:

1. New compensation systems that base pay on the scarcity and value of teachers' skills, the difficulty of their assignments, the extent of their responsibility, and the caliber of their work
2. Pension and healthcare benefits structured like those offered by other organizations (businesses) seeking to hire mobile, skilled, college-

educated professionals, which would end defined-benefit pension plans and "gold-plated" health insurance

3. Streamlined process for firing ineffective teachers and more flexibility in evaluating teachers

4. Assignment of teachers on the basis of educational need rather than seniority

5. Elimination of provisions related to work rules and governance with the union's role in crafting district policy limited to informal consultation

6. Ambiguous language on "managerial prerogatives" replaced by explicit language maximizing administration's flexibility (Hess and West 2006b)

The implementation of any and certainly all of these changes would negatively affect some teachers' work lives and positively affect others'. Our concern is where secondary science teachers will land if contracts are differentiated by performance as well as field, and this in turn will depend on who measures performance.

Report From the Field

Tom and Mary Anne are both secondary science teachers. Tom has taught middle-school science, as well as high-school biology and Earth science. He is currently a K–12 science supervisor with about 9,000 students in his district. And he lives in a state that not just permits teachers to join a union (the state NEA), but virtually requires them to do so.[7] Tom thinks his state is, in fact, the strongest union state in the country. It's a relatively small state with only 600 school districts, so not surprisingly, governors, senators, and local officials vie for endorsement from the state's NEA.

The NEA can't legally strike, but the teachers' collective political clout gets them the two- to three-year contracts they enjoy. Also, when frustrated, the union can have teachers "work the contract," that is, not do anything extra. The starting salary for teachers at any level in Tom's state—kindergarten or high-school physics—is $42,000 a year.

More than the money, Tom argues, are the "parameters of professionalism" that the union provides: "The union gives people a sense of shared direction and dedication." The downside is that in some districts (though the union will deny this), the union discourages teachers from doing any unpaid work such as Saturday science fairs. And, as far as professional development, outside of workshops provided by the district, Tom says, "You do this on your own time."

---

7. Thirty-seven states allow teachers to join a union, though none, technically, can require membership as a condition for employment. In some states that allow teachers' unions, a dues equivalent is deducted from the salaries of teachers who do not formally join, on the grounds that the union negotiates for them— so they must be "charged" for the benefits they receive, even if they refuse to join.

Mary Anne comes from a right-to-work state. No unions are permitted to represent teachers, no less to deduct dues from teachers' salaries. "Wages here are a lot lower than elsewhere. We start bachelors at $25,000 a year, but if you last the first year, you get a $1,000 bonus." Mary Anne interviewed the president of a nonunion teachers' organization in her state in preparation for our interview: "The president said she preferred our nonunion environment because she can build alliances that are not antagonistic."

Yet Mary Anne is clearly aware of the downside of not being represented by a union. "The teachers' association has been trying to work with the governor to guarantee teachers a duty-free lunch hour," she says, to take one example. "But my principal ignores that initiative, and the teachers are having lunch duty as before." As for class size, the teachers' association supposedly sets 24 pupils as the limit for a lab science. "But," says Mary Anne, "I can't really handle 24 at one time in a lab." The association's response: "We can't have different standards for science teachers." Twenty-four students it is.

In some states where unions are permitted, class size limits are part of the teachers' agreement. The National Science Teachers Association (NSTA), a membership organization, sets voluntary compliance for lab size, but this cannot be imposed.

With regard to professional development for science teachers, the contrast between union and nonunion states is stark. As science supervisor, Tom has a budget negotiated by the union to send 20 teachers a year to state meetings, covering teachers' overnight travel and meeting registration. But because those meetings are not part of the school calendar, any school principal or districtwide supervisor (including Tom) has the power to allow or refuse a teacher permission to go.

How much can and does the union protect individual teachers from harassment, from being unjustly let go? The union, Tom says, will support a teacher who feels he or she is being harassed. But nontenured teachers may be let go even with union support. The difference is this: "In my union state, you need to have a reason to fire a nontenured teacher," says Tom. "In a nonunion state, you don't even need that."

Conclusion

One of the several contradictions in the organization and management of schools in the United States, which bears directly on teacher-management relations, is that the teacher is both an employee of the superintendent of schools (represented by the school principal) and has a semiautonomous professional role within the classroom (see Cooper and Sureau 2008).

Contradictions arise because, given their classroom role, a "special work ethic" is attributed to teachers. One sociologist of school teaching in the early 1970s (before teachers' unions became large and active) described classroom teaching as having a "…dedicatory ethic which elevates service motives and denigrates material rewards" (Lortie 1975). Joining a union, then, may weaken the reputation of teachers, and turn teaching into just another job.

One way out of this dilemma is to argue that teachers are filling three roles at once: They are employees of their communities; in most jurisdictions, they are union members; and they are professionals seeking to apply their skills to the benefit of their students and their schools. But what if their school principal, their superintendent, or their school board doesn't agree? What recourse do they have to draw from?

References

Casey, L. 2007. The quest for professional voice. *The American Educator* (Summer). Also available online at *http://archive.aft.org/pubs-reports/american_educator/issues/summer07/casey.htm*

Connecticut State Association of Teachers. 2006. *Amicus brief in Connecticut et al. v. Margaret Spellings Sect'y of Education*, 549 F. Supp. 2d 459 (D), Conn.

Cooper, B. S., and J. Sureau. 2008. Teacher unions and the politics of fear in labor relations. *Educational Policy* 22 (1): 86–105.

Dillon, S. *New York Times*. 2007a. Long Reviled, Merit Pay Gains Among Teachers. June 17.

Dillon, S. *New York Times*. 2007b. With High Turnover, Schools Fight for Teachers. August 27.

Duffet, A., S. Farkas, A. J. Rotherman, and E. Silva. 2008. Waiting to be won over: Teachers speak on the profession, unions, and reform. *Education Sector Reports* (May).

Goldberg, S. *The Guardian*. 2005. US Judge Bans Intelligent Design From Science Lessons. December 21.

Gordon, R., T. J. Kane, and D. O. Staiger. 2006. Identifying effective teachers using performance on the job. Hamilton Project Discussion Paper 2006-01. Washington, DC: Brookings Institution. Also available online at *www.brookings.edu/~/media/Files/rc/papers/2006/04education_gordon/200604hamilton_1.pdf*

Hess, F. M., and M. R. West. *Boston Globe*. 2006a. Taking On the Teachers' Unions. March 29.

Hess, F., and West, M. 2006b. *A better bargain: Overhauling teacher collective bargaining for the 21st century*. Cambridge, MA: Program on Education Policy and Governance, Harvard University.

Hudson, S. P. 1986. Science teacher supply in the United States. *School Science and Mathematics* 96: 133–39.

Kahlenberg, R. D. 2007a. The agenda that saved public education. *The American Educator* (Fall).

Kahlenberg, R. D. 2007b. *Tough liberal: Albert Shanker and the battles over schools, unions, race, and democracy.* New York: Columbia University Press.

Kane, T. 2007. On point interview, May 3. Cambridge, MA: Project for Policy Innovation in Education, Harvard University.

Keller, B. 2006. NCLB law hasn't superseded contracts. *Education Week* (April 5): 8–9.

Leshner, A. I. *Houston Chronicle.* 2008. Board's Actions Could Put Students at a Disadvantage: Anti-Evolution Push May Hurt Efforts to Teach Science. October 22: B9.

Lortie, D. C. 1975. *Schoolteacher: A sociological study.* Chicago: University of Chicago Press.

Los Angeles Times. 2008. Obama's Well-Stocked Cabinet. December 28.

Mead, S. 2006. Teacher unions as agents of reform: An interview with Brad Jupp. *Education Sector Interviews* (April 18). Also available online at *www.educationsector.org/analysis/analysis_show.htm?doc_id=367110*

Medina, J. *New York Times.* 2008. Teachers to Be Measured Based on Students' Standardized Test Scores. October 1.

Missouri State Teachers Association. n.d. Teacher tenure act questions. *www.msta.org/faq/default.aspx?Cat_ID=119&Section=services*

Moulthrop, D., N. C. Calegari, and D. Eggers. 2006. *Teachers have it easy: The big sacrifices and the small salaries of America's teachers.* New York. W. W. Norton.

National Commission on Teaching & America's Future. 1996. *What matters most: Teaching for America's future.* New York: National Commission on Teaching & America's Future.

Navarrette, R. *San Diego Union-Tribune.* 2008. Great Choice for Education Secretary. December 24.

Patchogue-Medford Congress of Teachers. n.d. *Teacher tenure: Myths and realities.* Patchogue, NY: Patchogue-Medford Congress of Teachers.

Pettus, A. 2006. Grading teachers. *Harvard Magazine* (November–December). Also available online at http://harvardmagazine.com/2006/11/grading-teachers

Ricker, M. C. 2009. *Education Week webinar.* February 4.

Saunders, S. 2007. Tenure changes for new teachers are on the way. *New York Teacher* (December 3).

Sawchuk, S. 2008. Pay-for-tenure swap for D.C. teachers under debate. *Education Week* (August 27).

Sawchuk, S. 2009. Introduction to online chat. *Education Week* (February 9).

Small Newspaper Group. 2005. The hidden costs of tenure. *http://thehiddencostsoftenure.com*

Springer, M. 2009. Commentary. *Education Week webinar* (February 4).

Stewart, K. *Salt Lake Tribune.* 2009. Economy Brings Reprieve to Teacher Shortage. January 12.

Taylor, W. L., and C. Rosario. 2007. *Fresh ideas in collective bargaining: How new agreements help kids.* Washington, DC: Citizens' Commission on Civil Rights. Also available online at *www.cccr.org/downloads/FreshIdeas.pdf*

Toch. T., and R. Rothman. 2008. Rush to judgment: Teacher evaluation in public education. *Education Sector Reports* (January 29).

Wheeler, G. F. 2008. Science teachers' pay doesn't add up. *Education Week* (May 13).

Chapter 6

Ongoing Efforts to Elevate Teachers' Capability and Status

The publication of *A Nation at Risk: The Imperative for Educational Reform* in 1983 was more than just another report on the need for school reform. With its dramatic title and its incendiary language ("a rising tide of mediocrity"), the report was the first since the post-Sputnik era to link America's failing schools with an impending failure to compete globally. The new threat was Japan, South Korea, and Europe in the emerging tech-based knowledge economy rather than the military threat posed by the Soviet Union during the earlier period (National Commission on Excellence in Education 1983).[1] The report, which made the failures of U.S. schools very public, touched off a wave of local, state, and federal reform efforts. It could be argued that these culminated in the No Child Left Behind Act of 2002 (NCLB, see Chapter 4), though it is unlikely any of the commissioners who wrote *A Nation at Risk* would have approved NCLB.

---

1. Other examples of incendiary language include the following: "If an unfriendly power had attempted to impose on America the mediocre educational performance that exists today, we might well have viewed it as an act of war."

The "little blue book," as the report came to be called because it was so widely read and quoted, focused on high school and was noteworthy in recommending significantly higher and more rigorous standards for graduation, including a longer school day and a longer school year. Its call for "new basics," including four years of English and three years each of science and mathematics for all students, standardized tests of achievement, higher college admissions criteria, a seven-hour school day, and a 200- to 220-day school year, all made headlines. But for the authors, improving teachers' status, salaries, and standards in order to "attract and keep excellent candidates in the profession" was at least as important as setting higher standards for students. This translated into recommendations for higher starting salaries, an 11-month contract, more control by teachers over textbook selection, and continuous professional development (National Commission on Excellence in Education 1983).[2]

Yet, in *A Nation Reformed*, a 20-year retrospective of *A Nation at Risk*, David Gordon, the book's editor, finds the following:

> For all the time, money, and talk invested in reforms, the fundamental work of schools—classroom instruction—has not changed very much.... Educators have been treated as part of the problem, not part of the solution [and there has been] little or no focus on helping teachers and administrators improve their ability to perform the complex work that takes place in schools...including high-quality professional development. (Gordon 2003, p. 3)

In this chapter we will review a number of follow-ons to that strand in *A Nation at Risk* that focused on increasing teachers' performance and capability. Several have been in place long enough to measure their impact on teaching as a profession. Standing in the way of any reform are the conflicting political agendas at the state level and—the thesis of this book—the absence of classroom teachers in crafting educational policy overall. The result, as Pam Grossman, professor of education at Stanford, put it, reviewing *A Nation at Risk* in 2003, is that we have gone from "a nation at risk to a profession at risk."

---

2. The full list includes the following: more rigorous teacher preparation; higher salaries that are professionally competitive; salary, promotion, tenure and retention decisions tied to an effective peer review; 11-month contract for teachers; career ladders that distinguish among the beginning instructor, the experienced teacher, and the master teacher; incentive grants and loans; master teachers should be involved in designing teacher preparation programs and in supervising teachers during their probationary years.

States have tried to draw teachers in not by improving the conditions teachers work in and increasing professional development, but by relaxing the requirement for entry into the profession…policymakers continue to undermine efforts to professionalize teaching by creating conditions that lead to high turnover, burnout, and shoddy teacher standards. (Grossman 2003)

Efforts at school reform that don't succeed, David Gordon notes (in the selection quoted previously), tend to see teachers as part of the problem; hence the desire to fix *them*. Another misjudgment is to confound *empowerment* with *power*. Science teachers make this mistake, too, insofar as they allow professional administrators to operate in a vacuum, and teachers in other subject specialties to take charge. These points will be further elaborated in Chapter 9. We turn now to examining the impact on teachers and teaching of some reforms, that, unlike high-stakes testing, are designed to elevate teachers' status: National Board Certification, professional learning communities, and, in the next chapter, programs that partner science teachers with scientists.

Case 1: National Board Certification

One-hundred-and-fifty years ago, a group of professionals found themselves in a situation very much like that of science teachers today. Their occupation included a wide range of practitioners, having different levels of education, their practice based on different theories, and employing a wide and sometimes contradictory range of methods. We're describing here the mid–19th century medical profession in which highly educated and competent doctors competed with self-taught healers and out-and-out charlatans, all existing side by side, all claiming the title "doctor." As a result, the profession, like teaching today, enjoyed little privilege, respect, or reward.

To counter this state of affairs, in 1858, the American Medical Association (AMA) was formed. Its mission was to create codes of practice for the medical profession, to embrace ethical standards in the medical field, and to establish a means of disseminating information to members and to the public at large, in order to raise the professional status of doctors. Our question is this: Can science teaching ever achieve the elite professional status that physicians now enjoy? And if so, will it come through the imposition of national standards of practice?[3]

---

3. With regard to medicine, establishing standards was necessary but not sufficient. Real change involved changing medical education as well.

One group of educators thinks the answer to this question is "yes." A substantial effort has already been expended, and money spent—fast approaching $1 billion—on a proposed solution that in many ways mirrors the strategies employed by the AMA to "regularize" the medical profession. This strategy is called National Board Certification (Berg 2007).

What Is National Board Certification?

Not long after the publication of *A Nation at Risk*, and most likely in response to that book, the Carnegie Forum on Education and the Economy published a report, *A Nation Prepared: Teachers for the 21st Century*, calling for the creation of a board to "define what teachers should know and be able to do" (Carnegie Corporation 1986). Once these standards were agreed on, Carnegie proposed setting up "rigorous, valid assessments to see that certified teachers do meet those standards." One year later, with additional Carnegie Corporation funding, The National Board for Professional Teaching Standards (NBPTS) was established. The founding board, made up of teachers actively teaching in the classroom and chaired by former North Carolina Governor James B. Hunt, intended to elevate the professional status of teaching by laying out what an expert teacher should know and be able to do, in what the commission called "Five Core Propositions."[4]

NBPTS has been from the beginning a nonprofit, independent, and nongovernmental agency, and its National Board Certification the teaching profession's highest credential. Indeed, so far, 64,000 teachers (roughly 2% of the teaching force) have voluntarily undertaken the certification process to become National Board Certified Teachers (NBCTs). Their motivation? Certainly one element was the promise, then and now, that National Board Certification would result in stipends, higher salaries, or at the very minimum, one-time bonuses.

NBPTS offers 22 different certificates classified by 15 subject areas and 7 student age groups. With regard to science, teachers can certify in early adolescent science or adolescent and young adulthood science and must select one of the four science specialty areas:

- Biology
- Chemistry

---

4. The Five Propositions are: (1) Teachers are committed to students and their learning; (2) Teachers know the subjects they teach and how to teach those subjects to students; (3) Teachers are responsible for managing and monitoring student learning; (4) Teachers think systematically about their practice and learn from experience; and (5) Teachers are members of learning communities.

- Earth and space science
- Physics

Given the focus of this book, it is important to note that in the 20 years since NBPTS began offering certification, 7% of Nationally Board Certified Teachers have been in science, a fair representation.[5]

Requirements for Certification

The requirements for National Board Certification in any category are, by design, very rigorous and only 40% of first-time applicants pass on the first try. All candidates for certification must demonstrate their knowledge and skills by passing a written assessment and by creating a portfolio that documents the teachers' performance on the job.

The half-day written assessment for secondary science requires the candidate to demonstrate expertise in

- data analysis,
- interrelationships within a science,
- fundamental concepts in candidate's selected science discipline (biology, chemistry, Earth and space science, or physics),
- changes over time (biology, Earth and space science, and physics) or changes in systems (chemistry),
- connections in science, and
- breadth of knowledge across the major disciplines of science.

The portfolio must include

- one classroom-based entry with accompanying student work,
- two classroom-based entries that require video recordings of interactions between the teacher and his or her students, and
- one documented accomplishments entry that provides evidence of the teacher's accomplishments outside the classroom (with families, the community, or colleagues) and how that work impacts student learning.

Each portfolio entry is required to show direct evidence of teaching as well as a commentary describing, analyzing, and reflecting on the evidence.

---

5. The National Science Teachers Association estimates that there were approximately 180,000 (5.8% of all teachers) middle-school and secondary school science teachers actively teaching in the United States in 2007.

What Teachers Say About National Board Certification

We received varied responses to National Board Certification through interviews and website interactions with secondary science teachers who either held certification or had at one time considered pursuing it. Overall, the response of secondary science teachers is that the certification process requires something most teachers have very little of: time.

A science teacher from Florida writes that his National Board Certification took 100 hours more than the anticipated 200. A chemistry teacher from Missouri warns that the process is a three-year commitment. "Eliminate all other commitments from your schedule prior to beginning the process, and follow all directions to the letter," she advises.

As for whether the time required for certification is time well spent, many teachers echo this chemistry teacher from Alabama, who says,

> Doing certification provided one of the only times I have been able to reflect on what I do as a teacher, how I do things, and why I do them...and how all of it truly impacts my students and their learning.

An Oklahoma science teacher who spent two years working for her certification says of the process,

> It was grueling and stressful [yet] I would do it again in a heartbeat for what I have gained. I am a much-improved teacher now. I think about what I am teaching and why. I am more aware of the different activities and lessons that I teach and much more selective, [asking myself] How will it move my students forward? I also look at the whole student, [who is] taking other classes, extra-curricular, home, siblings, friends, jobs; what does that student need?

Others are more critical. One of teachers' chief complaints about the process is that it does nothing to relieve them of their isolation as professionals, both because teachers sign up for the three-year process individually (not as members of a school-based team), and because inadequate personal feedback further isolates the candidate.

Support systems have appeared recently to guide teachers through the NBPTS process, though none are formally endorsed by NBPTS. They include local mentoring by certified teachers of those just going through the process, to state and national networks that provide help online.

The Costs and the Payoff

Getting National Board Certification is not cheap (the price of the certificate is $2,500), but in many areas teachers can find help. The financial assistance and benefits vary widely from state to state and even from district to district.

Top Five and Bottom Five States by Total NBCTs and Financial Incentives Offered as of 2007

Top Five	Total	Financial Incentives
North Carolina	11,327	12% annual salary differential on base salary
Florida	9,236	10% annual salary bonus plus 10% for mentoring
South Carolina	5,076	$7,500 annual salary supplement
California	3,656	$20,000 over four years in a high-priority school
Ohio	2,629	$2,500 annual stipend (before 2004; $1,000 after 2004)

Bottom Five	Total	Financial Incentives
South Dakota	59	$2,000 for at least five years
Montana	58	$3,000 one-time stipend
Nebraska	48	—
North Dakota	26	$1,500 for four years mentoring
New Hampshire	17	

Note: NBCTs in these states may be eligible for additional financial incentives from local districts or other local sources (Berg 2007).

Dollar rewards and reimbursement vary not only by state but also by state administration. One biology teacher from Georgia found the state initially willing to pay 10% over and above her normal salary, "but that changed when the governor changed."

The state of North Carolina pays the application fees for all eligible teachers and increases the salary of National Board Certified teachers by 12%. But a more common practice is for a state to offer partial financial assistance with application fees and annual stipends that range from $500 to $5,000.

Does Board Certification Result in Increased Professional Status?

A key question, especially for our inquiry, is whether National Board Certification results in increased professional status for the teachers who complete the requirements. The problem is that while "national" in its standards for certification, acknowledgment and rewards are determined by local boards and school administrators. In the one case, as reported by a New Jersey biology teacher, "acknowledgement" was only perfunctory: "The district did give me a little plaque, and I was invited to a state board of education meeting to get another little plaque, but really the only benefits come from what I learned about myself." But a physics teacher from Wisconsin found that it did add another layer to his professionalism. Obviously, we want to see more of that.

One long-time board certified teacher remembers, "My principal didn't even acknowledge the accomplishment because he had no idea what it meant." Part of the problem was that the teacher was the first in his district to be board certified. Another is that National Board Certification has not made itself widely understood. Reports a middle-school science teacher from Texas, "They think you paid your money and got your certification. They have no idea how demanding the process is."

Yet, according to a Missouri biology teacher, "Board certification is, I believe, one of the reasons I was chosen as an Albert Einstein Distinguished Educator Fellow and received the Presidential Award for Excellence in Math and Science Teaching."

Things were about to change.

The Impact of No Child Left Behind on National Board Certification

During the 1990s, five years after most states had already made a major investment in National Board Certification, three large-scale studies were published that for the first time specifically addressed the impact of Board-Certified teachers on student achievement test scores (Berg 2007). Finding that students of teachers with board certification performed better on average than students with non–Board-Certified teachers, these early studies initiated a new wave of support for board certification. As a result, by 2004, all 50 states and more than 700 school districts were participating in National Board Certification. Funding structures also favored special allocations or stipends for Board-Certified teachers.

But by 2005, scores from the newly conceived high-stakes testing required by NCLB (see Chapter 4) challenged the earlier findings. Maybe certified teachers did not outperform non–National Board Certified peers. A shift in focus followed. Where "teacher quality" had previously been assumed to be an intrinsic set of skills, attitudes, and experience, together with a willingness to learn and improve, now "teacher quality" devolved into one measure: that of student "improvement" as calculated by test scores. And, ominously, studies began to appear showing that board-certified teachers were no more "effective" in raising student test scores than those who were not board certified.

According to Charles Coble, a former dean of education at the University of North Carolina, "The [new high-stakes] tests are not sensitive to the effects of National Board Certification." But what accounts, we ask him, for the initial boost of test scores followed by no real difference? "Natural statistical regression," Coble explains, referring to the greatly expanded number of National Board Certified teachers following increased state rewards for obtaining board certification. Indeed, the number of such teachers had nearly tripled during that five-year period.

Despite these numerical gains and the spread of National Board Certification to all 50 states, in an NCLB regime, the program may be in serious jeopardy. Witness the 2007 National Action Plan of the National Science Board, which calls for "national STEM teacher certification guidelines," but explicitly not National Board Certification (National Science Board 2007, p. 21). Another indication that National Board Certification may fall to the NCLB's single criterion of pupils' improvement in test scores is that in June 2008, the Florida State Legislature cut funding in half for its Board Certified teacher program by eliminating the 10% bonus for mentoring new teachers and the subsidy that helped teachers cover $150 in portfolio expenses and 90% of the $2,500 application fee. Other states are threatening to follow Florida's lead.

Case 2: Professional Learning Communities (PLCs)

A central element of a profession is the proposition that participants both train and become certified *before* being given responsibility in their work environment, and that they *continue to learn* and to be updated throughout their careers. *Preservice* is the term given to precertification requirements for teachers; *inservice* or *professional development* is what's required or recommended throughout their careers. All teachers need to upgrade their pedagogical skills, and because their fields are moving so swiftly, secondary science teachers need as well to have a general knowledge of advances in their fields. All of which more than justify some time spent away from the classroom.

So far so good. But what concerns us is how the educational community applies the word *professional*. Our teacher respondents have directed us to look critically at elements that enhance or detract from professional status. So the question we bring to the current state of professional development is whether these programs enhance teachers' professional standing or only—however important this may be—teachers' ability to be effective instructors.

The problems with "professional development" from the science teachers' point of view have until now been two: first, the generic or one-size-fits all approach that casts secondary science teachers in an audience for professional training that includes elementary, social studies, health, and foreign language teachers. The second is the use of outside consultants who do not know local conditions.

We are not the first to have observed this. Teachers, both science and nonscience, have been complaining about the inservice practice for decades. So there's a new model, borrowed from business, having to do with how working conditions affect employees. Education scholar Shirley Hord and others have applied this new model to the school and named it the *professional learning community* (PLC). A PLC is designed to engage teachers and their administrators not only in substantive discussion about curriculum and pedagogy but in occasional collective decision making, which is, of course, not possible when an outside consultant is called in.

When experiments with learning communities started in the 1980s and 1990s, it was noted that teachers who felt supported in their learning and practice appeared more committed and effective than those who were not participating in learning communities. And even better news was that teachers with a strong sense of efficacy were more likely to innovate in the classroom and stay in the field (Rosenholtz 1989). Other researchers confirmed the fact that when teachers collaborate in learning about teaching, and have a voice in curricular issues, they are stronger. Moreover, their schools are better. Schools that provide time for teacher collaboration and shared decision making appeared highly "effective."[6]

If Shirley Hord is the creator of the term *professional learning community*, Richard DuFour, an award-winning Illinois district superintendent, and Robert Eaker, a college of education dean, are its champions. The team presents workshops across the United States for thousands of teachers and administrators ready to launch learning communities at their schools. For teachers, participating in a learning community means both changing the

---

6. These findings were rooted in concepts developed by private sector researchers such as Senge (1990), Drucker (1999), and Covey (1989), who increasingly focused on collaborative problem-solving activities as keys to vibrant and efficient companies, which they called "learning organizations."

content and changing the way professional development is delivered. Instead of attending an off-site workshop, teachers in a learning community meet at their school in small teams to learn and work together on improving teaching and learning. They identify common goals, review the latest research on teaching and learning, collaboratively design a research-based curriculum, and develop methods for assessing the results of that curriculum in the classroom. Learning communities allow teachers to steep themselves in teaching practice.

Members of a well-functioning learning community might study student work, analyze the components of a skill they want to develop in their students, and create new instructional approaches and assessments to address gaps in student performance. As the learning community proceeds, it would collect data from students and from one another to assess the progress their students are making over a specific period of time. Teachers in a high-school science learning community, meeting every week during a common planning period, might decide to explore ways to help their students write better conclusions to their lab reports.

In a learning community, teachers learn new skills together instead of in isolation: "Educators have typically been isolated physically from others because of the structure of school facilities and the schedules that dominate the school day" (Hord and Sommers 2008, p. 1).

But this can work both ways. Some teachers we interviewed indicated that the independence and autonomy of teaching in their own classrooms is part of what drew them to the field. Yet now they're being asked to work together in a schoolwide effort to affect student learning, which may not be their best "learning style." In fact, the "mavericks" on staff resent spending time with other teachers figuring out what to do in their own classrooms.

At least as revolutionary as an inservice conducted *by* as well as *for* teachers, is the shift in the role of the principal. If a learning community is to succeed in its decision-making function, to paraphrase DuFour, the culture of the school has to move from command and control to one of support and collaboration (DuFour 2004).

Obstacles: Lack of Time and Lack of Trust

There is ample evidence that an effective learning community can help teachers refine their lessons and improve student learning. But does it make for a better professional experience for the teachers themselves? Unless it does, many teachers will decide that a learning community may not be worth the cost of even more time away from the classroom.

Teachers have learned to cram in as much as possible and still try to teach well. As we've seen, those who want to use inquiry-based methods have to put in more time—developing the inquiry lessons, setting up the classroom for the work, preparing students to handle the new environment. So adding one more assignment can be quite unpopular.

Apparently, learning communities work best when the meetings occur during the school day, providing teachers with "extra time" for the collaboration. Some options for creating time for learning communities include the following:

- Extending four days each week for instruction, then providing an early release day for students, with teachers remaining in the building to meet. This requires community buy-in and usually union approval.

- Using staff development funds to hire substitutes who cover classes so teachers can meet.

- Devoting departmental meetings to learning community work and using e-mail to take care of departmental administrative details.

Most high schools cannot make these changes all at once and some not at all. When learning communities are initiated without sufficient time, they become an imposition and a burden.

As for the content of a learning community discussion, our interviewees tell us the devil is in the details. What exactly is meant by "teacher collaboration?" What is the difference between complaining about a student and seriously discussing what type of learning environment will best serve that student? The key to successful learning communities is when their collaborative activities meet the needs of the individual science teacher.

What Science Teachers Say About Professional Learning Communities

When we posted some questions about PLCs on our website, we heard a range of comments about whether learning communities contribute to teacher professionalism or are used for other purposes. A science chair in Arizona—our most prolific respondent—tells us that in her district, school is dismissed early every Wednesday to provide time for what is officially called "staff development." But because it is the only time available for department business meetings, full-faculty meetings, department curriculum development, and interdepartmental discussion, the time is often usurped to meet some higher priority need mandated at the district or administrative level.

Mostly the learning community time at her school does not focus on learning activities. She writes,

> Since the school (and every school in the district) has been designated a professional learning community, any momentary cluster of three or more people in the same space is deemed a PLC and thus can be counted as evidence of our site commitment to the PLC model. So when department chairs and administrators attend the weekly Instructional Council meeting to discuss policy issues, it is now considered a PLC. When the science department has a business meeting to wade through supply orders and budget issues, we are of course doing it as a PLC. When everything is a called a PLC, is anything *really* a PLC?

It is possible that some teachers do not need much training to work effectively as a learning community. The Arizona science chair continues,

> My department *has always been* a genuine professional learning community, perhaps simply by virtue of the fact that we are by nature analytical, experimental, collaborative, and purely fascinated by how people learn. Science teachers like nothing better than to share 'best practice,' and we were doing it long before that catch phrase existed.

Like every other innovation, professional learning communities can be abused. Unfortunately, in some schools, the learning communities' agendas are hypermanaged by school administrators. That's when teachers' professionalism is lost. Teachers want to compare themselves with other professionals, like architects or doctors, who meet and exchange ideas, and are then free to accept or reject the practices learned in these meetings. This is as it should be because professionals are held individually responsible for their performance. "Too often in overly scripted learning communities, teachers lose this freedom to accept or reject certain practices," one chemistry teacher laments.

How can learning communities be made to better serve teachers' professional development? One answer comes from Shirley Hord, who first explored PLCs. A crucial variable for Hord is the willingness of the principal to share power by inviting staff input into decision making (Hord and Sommers 2008). Because this is rarely the case, we judge the learning community model to be only part of the answer, if other factors come into play. What if teachers were paid for their learning community time? What if they participated in research experiences and came back and shared their professional growth in teams? That might serve the science teachers' professional status and needs more profoundly.

The Other Shoe: Teacher Education

National Board Certification and professional learning communities were efforts to enhance teachers' effectiveness *before* No Child Left Behind was implemented. The question is: Will any of these survive the new single focus on pupils' incremental progress as the only measure of teacher effectiveness? A key player will be those responsible for teacher education because high-stakes testing not only devalues teachers' independence but also their certification. Recall the Brookings study (see Chapter 1) that would replace teacher certification altogether with that single measure. One more lesson can be taken from the strides made by the medical profession, with which analogy this chapter began. The standards for practice set by the AMA in the late 19th century turned out to be insufficient to drive out the charlatans and quacks from the practice of medicine. Medical education itself had to change.

Again the Carnegie Foundation took the lead, assigning a study in 1914 to Abraham Flexner, an educator (not a physician). In record time (critics of Flexner say too fast), Flexner traveled to and closely examined 155 medical schools, where he found many institutions inadequate in the training of doctors; others no more than "diploma mills." He recommended a new (in fact the first real) standard of medical education: two full years of lab science followed by two full years of training in clinical practice, all in the hands of nationally qualified medical educators. Eventually, all of Flexner's recommendations came to pass: Undergraduate medical schools were abandoned in favor of the higher-level postgraduate medical education that stands today.

Are the elevated standards inherent in National Board Certification and in the work of teachers engaged in professional learning communities being incorporated into our teacher education centers? Are we ready for standardizing teacher education? If not overall, then at least in STEM?

These are the questions that should direct the next round of reform.

References

Berg, J. H. 2007. Resources for reform: The role of board-certified teachers in improving the quality of teaching, PhD diss., Graduate School of Education, Harvard University.

Carnegie Corporation. 1986. *A nation prepared: Teachers for the 21st century.* The report of the Task Force on Teaching as a Profession. Hyattsville, MD: Carnegie Forum on Education and the Economy.

Covey, S. R. 1989. *The 7 habits of highly effective people.* New York: Simon & Schuster.

Drucker, P. F. 1999. *Management challenges for the 21st century.* New York: HarperCollins.

DuFour, R. 2004. Schools as learning communities. *Educational Leadership* 61 (8): 6–11.

Gordon, D. ed. 2003. *A nation reformed? American education 20 years after* A Nation at Risk. Cambridge, MA: Harvard Education Press.

Grossman, P. 2003. Teaching: From a nation at risk to a profession at risk? In *A nation reformed? American education 20 years after* A Nation at Risk, ed. D. Gordon, 69–97.

Hord, S., and W. Sommers. 2008. *Leading professional learning communities: Voices from research and practice.* Thousand Oaks, CA: Corwin.

National Commission on Excellence in Education. 1983. *A nation at risk: The imperative for educational reform.* Washington, DC: U.S. Government Printing Office.

National Science Board. 2007. *National action plan for addressing the critical needs of the U.S. science, technology, engineering, and mathematics.* Arlington, VA: National Science Foundation.

Rosenholtz, S. 1989. *Teachers' workplaces: The social organization of the schools.* New York: Longman.

Senge, P. M. 1990. *The fifth discipline: The art & practice of the learning organization.* New York: Doubleday.

Chapter 7

Engaging Science Teachers in the Wider World of Science

Much of the impetus for school reform after 1983 was designed to enhance the nation's math/science "report card." Yet, as we have seen in Chapter 6, efforts to enhance teachers' competency and status tended to be subject unspecific. National Board Certification is an exception. While it qualifies teachers of all subjects and all levels, subject-specific certifications in science are provided, within the broader sweep of "board certification." Professional learning communities, on the other hand, while having the potential to serve teachers in a single subject area more often, are school based with teachers in all subject areas invited to confer about topics that go beyond any one subject's curriculum and instruction.

For science teachers, there are, of course, National Science Foundation teacher workshops and the National Science Teachers Association (NSTA), which provides its 60,000 members with a range of services including journals, newsletters, and the privilege of attending three regional meetings and one national meeting per year, devoted to the subjects they teach and to their needs.[1] But apart from going back to a university for an advanced degree in their science, how can secondary science teachers remain connected—as professionals—to science and scientists?

It did not take us long to locate four programs designed to do this, all based on a similar rationale, namely, that secondary science teachers need to experience real science, working at the bench, at the computer, and in a structured collaboration with other scientists.

---

1. In addition, NSTA has helped to advance a number of professional development programs.

The Partners Project

One of these programs was launched in 1988 by Research Corporation for Science Advancement (RCSA) in Tucson, Arizona. Called the "Partners Project," over a 10-year period, RCSA staff selected 376 high-school teachers of science from a national competition, assigned them to 372 mentors and got them summer research positions in 117 colleges and universities in 19 states. Twenty-two foundations partnered with RCSA, which made it possible for the foundation to provide significant summer stipends to the teacher-researchers. The program began modestly with 30 teacher-researchers and peaked in 1994 when 120 were placed.

In 1999 the M. J. Murdoch Charitable Trust took over RCSA's program, called it the Partners in Science program (or PiS), and refocused recruitment on high-school teachers of science in the Pacific Northwest. Within five years, Murdoch had added another 234 teacher-researchers (and 204 different mentors) to the roster, drawing from 173 high schools of the region's 1,150. As many as 34% of a single state's (Oregon's) high schools have participated over the years in PiS, the average across all five Pacific Northwest states being 13% (M. J. Murdock Charitable Trust n.d.).

Teacher stipends are an important part of both the RCSA and PiS programs. Murdoch teachers make a base commitment for two summers of research in a college or university lab. In exchange, the teacher earns a $5,000 stipend per summer plus $2,000 for travel, professional enrichment, and research or teaching. Thus, in a two-year period, a high-school science teacher can augment his or her pay by $10,000, and take home an additional $4,000 for materials, travel, and other ways of enriching his or her students' experience.

During their "Partners" summers, the teacher-researchers are not only involved in laboratory research, but also sit in on courses in such areas as DNA/biotechnology, molecular biology, computer interfacing, and environmental science. They work in environmental research, computer "probe ware" physics, and chemistry labs. The benefit of networking with scientists and other science teachers does not end with their summer labs. Because they are working in nearby universities, PiS teachers can and do bring their students to their mentors' labs, participate in on-campus events, and invite their mentors to their schools. But just as valuable, the Partners tell us, is their continued contact with science teachers from other high schools.

In a survey of teacher-researchers conducted by the Murdoch Trust in 2004, to measure the impact of the two research summers on their teaching, participating teachers reported "more effective and relevant teaching," that they are able "to initiate research opportunities for students in their classrooms" and "to connect them with scientists in the field." Most salient for our analysis, many say they "now teach with a firsthand understanding of doing science" (M. J. Murdock Charitable Trust 2004). With regard to their self-perception as professionals, Murdoch's teachers report they have increased self-esteem, a new (or renewed) perception of themselves as scientists, and a sense of professionalism, together with a boost to their morale.

Is there evidence of changes in the students they teach (the top and bottom line for policy makers)? The Partners point to four: (1) increased enrollment in elective science courses, (2) increase in the number of seniors interested in a science major in college or a career in science, (3) time spent by students in scientists' labs, and (4) increased participation in science competitions.

How many partners in how many additional areas of the United States does it take for a model to become a movement? The model for PiS appears to be widely applicable when money is available.[2] In addition to the 234 teachers funded by the Murdoch Trust from 1998 to 2003, another 118 science teachers from 94 high schools spent two summers working with 100 mentors at local universities. And, as of summer 2009, RCSA is back, partnering this time with the Murdoch Trust.

California's STAR Program

The Science Teacher and Researcher (STAR) program was the brainchild of Warren Baker, president of one of California State University's premier science and engineering campuses, at San Luis Obispo. Baker has also been cochair of the Business Higher Education Forum (BHEF), whose concern is "securing America's leadership in science, technology, engineering and mathematics." In testimony before the U.S. Congress in September 2007, Baker described the "Teacher-Scientist model" as one that will introduce science majors to a dual career as teacher during the academic year and paid science researcher in the summer (Baker 2007). But while intended initially to increase the number and quality of STEM majors aiming to be secondary teachers, the STAR program now includes teacher candidates and working science and mathematics teachers early in their careers, as well.

Indeed, with support from the National Science Foundation and participation of the Lawrence Livermore National Laboratory (LLNL), the program quickly expanded to include the National Labs at Berkeley, Sandia/California, the Stanford Linear Accelerator Center (SLAC), and the NASA

---

2. At time of writing, the Murdoch Trust's outlay has totaled $4.3 million.

Ames Research Center. STAR participants receive $4,000 for summer research internships in federal laboratories where they join ongoing research teams.[3] As the program expands still more, STAR will provide additional opportunities for internships in industry and university labs, and in time add more beginning teachers to its pool.

In its first pilot summer (2007), 16 STAR participants worked with scientists at LLNL on a wide variety of projects. (LLNL is no longer doing only nuclear/weapons work.)[4] They also participated in seminars to "explicitly connect the doing of science to the teaching of science in the classroom" (STAR 2008). The connection with classroom teaching is never far from center stage during the STAR summer research experience. Questions like, How might you illustrate the practice of conducting scientific research to students? and, How might you help students understand how the practice of science works? are explicitly posed during the seminars.

Fearful that the experience of doing real science with scientists might have deflected participants from their choice of teaching as a career, one of the authors of this book (Tobias) conducted interviews with all 16 at the conclusion of their summer projects and found not one any less committed to teaching than before. Rather, they were being inducted into science at the same time they were being inducted into teaching, forging—as one of the program's avid proponents puts it—their identity as teacher/scientists. It is for this reason, too, that educators currently teaching chemistry and physics are being recruited to serve as master teachers or guest lecturers in the summer sessions, to demonstrate the natural links between teaching and research. The master teachers, just as their mentees, will receive summer stipends along with exposure to the workings of a national lab.

The finding from a second-year evaluation is especially relevant to the themes of this book. Even one summer in a working laboratory can serve to expand teachers' and future teachers' professional identity, or, as described in the STAR Final Report, make them feel they have a place in the scientific community (STAR 2008). As of this writing, aspiring and early career teachers in the California State University (CSU) system have access to summer research intern programs at five different Department of Energy (DOE) and NASA research sites in the Bay Area. Additional funding is provided by two foundations (Bechtel, Fluor) and the Raytheon Company.

---

3. In addition to the $4,000 stipend for eight weeks of work, participants may claim up to $3,000 in travel and living expenses if the National Lab is more than commuting distance from their home.

4. The National Labs, which began as weapons laboratories during World War II, are now engaged in a full spectrum of scientific investigation at the forefronts of science, technology, and engineering.

DOE hosts two other programs with the same general thrust. For more experienced teachers seeking an independent research experience with a mentor scientist, there are a series of small "academies" (see *http:// education.llnl.gov/doeacts/*). DOE also offers preservice teachers summer work in a national lab. According to DOE's Pre-Service Teacher website (*www.scied.science.doe.gov/scied/pst/about.htm*), participants are expected to work more than 40 hours per week over a 10-week period and to submit a research paper along with—and this is significant in that it links the research activity with their future teaching—an "education module," presumably a planning document about how they will adapt the research topic they worked on all summer to their teaching. Thus is DOE fully invested in accommodating a wide range of teachers' desire to interact with working scientists.

What is the future of these programs? Will other federal agencies participate? Can DOE expand theirs to accommodate thousands instead of hundreds of teachers? According to Bill Valdez of the science department at DOE, in a personal communication to the authors, "the Agency intends to try to expand the model to states other than California." Other agencies are "intrigued" by the approach, but he says, DOE is especially appropriate.

> DOE is blessed with scientists who are willing to work with K–12 teachers, an asset that many other agencies do not have. …[Still] it is possible that other federal agencies will be interested in the STAR model because currently there is no other model in government.[5]

Florida Programs for Preservice and Inservice Teachers in Research

Proof that this model is propagating are the programs at Florida State University (FSU) and University of Florida (UF) that also link teachers with working scientists. At UF, science, math, and technology teachers spend the summer working on campus with scientists (see Barnes et al. 2006). At FSU, Penny Gilmer, professor of science education, arranges scientific research experiences for practicing K–8 teachers. Instead of requiring them to come to Tallahassee, teachers are encouraged to collaborate with scientists who work near their schools. As with the other programs described in this chapter, the teachers very soon become "scientists."

---

5. Bill Valdez, personal communication to the authors.

One teacher reports, "A firsthand experience doing scientific research and the opportunity to interact with scientists in the field, gave me the confidence and the ability to incorporate multiple areas of science into my teaching" (Greenspan 1999).

The FSU program is also available for preservice teachers, to give them a scientific research experience as soon as possible in their careers. A prospective biology teacher, reflecting on the experience writes, "I grasped the concepts of biology more profoundly when I analyzed an ecosystem in its natural habitat. Neither textbook nor traditional laboratory could compare with experiencing science as it occurs in nature" (Gilmer 2002, p. 20)

A third related effort links FSU with the Panhandle Area Educational Consortium (PAEC; see *www.paec.org*) to provide research experiences for rural teachers throughout northwestern Florida. Teachers conduct scientific research near their home or school with scientists who work at state parks, estuarine reserves, tortoise reserves, a marine laboratory, and a state agricultural lab. An important feature of this program is teaming elementary-, middle- and high-school teachers with the scientists (Calvin and Gilmer 2008).

Industry Initiatives for Science and Mathematics Education (IISME)

Older by far than any of the programs described previously is California's Industry Initiatives for Science and Mathematics Education (IISME) project for working teachers in the San Francisco and Sacramento areas. IISME teachers (usually with at least eight years' teaching experience) are provided summer fellowships for work in what are called "high-performance work sites." They are able to earn up to $900 per week plus $1,000 in fellowship grants from employers who wish to serve themselves as well as education in a program that is typically seven weeks long. Teachers complete a project for their sponsors and also spend time focusing on ways to transfer their summer fellowship experience back to their students and colleagues. It helps significantly that they can speak with more authority about the kind of work science majors will find in business and industry, when they talk about "careers in science" with their students.

As of this writing, more than 1,500 California teachers have participated in IISME programs. The teachers are provided hands-on, practical as-

signments intended to confer a better understanding of the skill requirements needed in the modern workplace. The skills and insights they gain
on the job are, of course, theirs to keep, but so are the relationships they
forge with their employers, which tend to be long-term. Meanwhile, host
employers get mature, seasoned temporary employees to work on a specific
task or problem. Additionally, the employer gets the new perspective of an
external hire, benefits to the employer's own image within the community, and the chance to make a contribution to education. (See *www.iisme.
org?AboutSummerFellowships.cfm* for more information.)

Because IISME has been in operation since 1985, the impact of the program on teacher attrition can be evaluated. Compared with a national average
of 8% annual departure of teachers, IISME fellows leave teaching at the rate
of 4% (leaving education overall at the rate of 2%). When asked on question-
naires whether IISME serves as an impetus to stay in teaching, 329 of the for
mer fellows still in education respond "yes" (Weisbaum and Huang 2001).

The teachers' impact on student learning is higher, according to IISME
participants themselves, than from any other professional development
experience the teachers may have had. More of their students participate
in Intel Science Talent Searches and more join science clubs in their high
schools. Also, of particular interest from our perspective, a higher proportion of IISME teachers enroll in (or were already certified by) National
Board Certification.

What Science Teachers Say About Summer Research Opportunities

We were not able to interview the many hundreds of RCSA's "Partners" or,
except for the first precertified cohort, any of the summer STAR teacher-
researchers, and none of the IISME teachers. But we were able to interview
a number of the Murdoch Trust's Partners in Science, teaching in Portland,
Oregon. Here is what they remember about the program and its impact on
their teaching.

> **Nancy:** I had never had a research experience before this one. It rein-
> forced why I want to teach rather than do research…. When, after two
> summers, I found myself working at the same level as the postdocs in the
> lab, and finding errors in their papers, that gave me more self-confidence
> in my abilities to do science…outside the classroom.

Mike: I was working at the Primate Center, looking for neuropeptides in brain tissue. I felt like I was actually contributing something to the research.

Charles: My students were aware what I was doing and when one of my students asked, "What's the point of all this?" I used the question as a subtitle of a presentation. [At the lab] I spent hours looking at a microscope. Now I create three- or four-day labs that force my students to think about what they're doing. Probably the most valuable thing I ever did for my teaching.

Steve: All of a sudden you have credibility because you've done science! And when your school district buys in, they have invested in you. PiS is where I blossomed professionally. It was a springboard for me.

Larry: My PiS experience changed how I teach. My labs became more inquiry based. I get my kids to focus on: What do we want to know? What's the focus that we want?

Colleen: I did not really know what science is until I did PiS. In the atmospheric chemistry lab, I was amazed how long it takes to collect knowledge and how many people are involved. This taught me to slow down and to focus more on asking questions in the classroom; to listen more to students' ideas.

Ten years after her two PiS summers, Colleen is still presenting papers and workshops on the subject of her summer research and is paid for her travel. She comments, "There aren't many perks in teaching. It's all intrinsic, so it's nice to have someone on the outside to value you."

The Kenan Fellows Program

The Kenan Fellows Program was established in 2000 in North Carolina's Research Triangle as a part of a community effort to retain effective math and science teachers. The founders of the Kenan Foundation for Curriculum and Leadership Development were well aware of the twin issues that we have been tracking in this book: the critical role that strong STEM (science, technology, engineering, and math) teachers play in readying the next generation to compete in the global economy, and the importance of not losing the most skilled of these teachers to attrition. A survey of North Carolina teachers completed in 2006 showed incontrovertibly that school leadership and teachers' sense of empowerment were strongly related to teacher attrition (Hirsch et al. 2006). In a word, teachers who felt empowered were less likely to leave teaching.

What the Kenan Foundation decided to try was to link teachers' professional development with leadership training as a way to keep top science and math teachers in the system. U.S. Rep. David Price (D-NC) spotlighted the Kenan Program in June 2007, when he introduced his "Keep Teachers Teaching Act," as an example of a promising statewide effort in teacher retention.[6]

The Kenan Fellows Program is administered by the Kenan Institute for Engineering, Technology and Science at North Carolina State University. At the time of writing, there are 95 fellows in the program (66 have successfully completed the program and 29 entered in 2008). While fellows' projects must have a STEM focus, the lessons can be delivered across other content areas. A few visual arts and career/technology teachers, as well as some academically gifted specialists, have been admitted to the program, but math and science teachers make up two-thirds of the fellows, with biology, chemistry, and physics being the most frequently represented.

Outstanding classroom teachers compete for this fellowship, which includes a $10,000 stipend, use of a laptop computer, and graduate credit in addition to funds to attend conferences. School administrators, community leaders, parents of students and former Kenan fellows may nominate candidates. Once selected, they enter into a two-year program (part time) that partners them with scientists and university faculty to develop innovative curriculum out of current and applied research topics in science. During their fellowship, these high-school teachers work in tandem with and enjoy the status of academic researchers. They present their work at national and international conventions. With their mentors, they coauthor articles, publish research, and apply for grant funding.

Not unlike the thinking that underlies the Partners and the STAR programs, the expectation is that once exposed to cutting-edge science research, high-school teachers will return to their classrooms newly invigorated and will inspire their students by showing them how to apply their academic knowledge to solving authentic, real-life problems.

Capacity building is not limited to new curricula and new modes of instruction. Mindful of the need to further empower these selected teacher leaders, the Kenan program trains them to navigate the educational policy-making world. Or, as Kenan Fellows Director Valerie Brown-Schild explains, "They learn how to talk to policy makers." The program created "fireside chats" where fellows interact with education, government, and corporate leaders who are responsible for making decisions about education. Fellows are also trained and encouraged to write op-ed pieces.

---

6. Keep Teachers Teaching Act (H.R. 2903), provides federal grants directly to states or school districts to develop innovative teacher retention programs. This bill has been incorporated into draft legislation to reauthorize and reform the No Child Left Behind Act, which is due for renewal.

During one of these fireside chats with North Carolina Sen. Vernon Malone in 2007, fellows presented a research-based document detailing teacher-retention problems and proposed solutions that included increased state funding for programs like the Kenan Fellows Program.

Eventually, Kenan Fellows are expected to return to their high schools and revitalize their colleagues by providing new insights into how they might connect to educational policy makers, researchers, and business leaders. With the program so young, its actual impact remains to be seen.

The fellows are indeed a very distinguished group of teachers well on their way to becoming the educational leaders of the future. Since beginning their fellowships,

- 61% have received awards such as "Teacher of the Year,"

- 56% have been awarded grants, and

- 96% have engaged in leadership activities such as appointments to the North Carolina Environmental Education Advisory Board and the High School Reform Committee for Durham Public Schools.

According to one fellow, "My teacher leadership training has been enhanced by my becoming more aware and informed regarding issues that directly affect classrooms, yet are not areas where teachers regularly have input (assessment programs, curriculum, educational policy, and teacher retention).

Another fellow writes, "The interaction with [state] leaders gave me the confidence to believe my ideas mattered and that I could effect change at any level."

During the past few years, the program has expanded its targeted geographic area to include all of North Carolina and now includes some teachers from more economically disadvantaged areas that have traditionally had high teacher turnover rates and poorer student achievement.

Conclusion

What should we make of the "teacher-scientist" model of professional development? Is it, as some of the participants and all of the funders suggest, the best way to expand the horizons of the science teacher? Herself a scientist-turned-administrator, Shirley Malcom, director of Education and Human Resources at the American Association for the Advancement of Science (AAAS) in Washington, D.C., notes that secondary science teachers gain more than the upgrading of their skills and knowledge that comes from doing research in a professional setting. In addition, they gain a referent group of other scientists to relate to. The designation as a "teacher-scientist" or "teacher-researcher" enhances their own professional identity and reminds them that as they provide information for the students in their classroom, they also can and do serve as models for them of the ways scientists think and do science. Dr. Malcom elaborates,

> It is very hard to teach the nature of science if you haven't really experienced it—going from a question to hypotheses, development to literature review, to design of experiments and so on. Being in a research setting forces [teachers] to confront certain myths that pervade common views of science and scientists: that we work alone in a solitary pursuit of knowledge; that we seldom consider the impact of the work on society and so on. Science teachers are on the frontlines of the enterprise but seldom relate to scientists as colleagues. In a lab or field setting, when they are suddenly contributing members of a team, when they are coauthors on journal articles, when they offer insights on solving problems or prove to have valuable communications and teaching skills, they are forced to view themselves differently.[7]

And, according to our informants, they do. Malcom goes on,

> I don't see this as professional development so much as *profession* development, reinforcing the view that as a teacher of science one has multiple reference groups—a critical step in recognizing one's value within the society.

References

Baker, W. 2007. Testimony before the U.S. House Committee on Education and Labor. Higher Education, Lifelong Learning, and Competitiveness Subcommittee. September 21.

Barnes, M. B., E. M. Hodge, M. Parker, and M. J. Koroly. 2006. The teacher research update experience: Perceptions of practicing science, mathematics, and technology teachers. *Journal of Science Teacher Education* 17 (3): 243–64.

Calvin, K., and P. J. Gilmer. eds. 2008. *Real science for the real world: Doing, learning, and TEACHING!* Chipley, FL: Panhandle Area Educational Consortium. Also available online at *www.chem.fsu.edu/~gilmer/*

Gilmer, P. J. 2002. Impact of scientific research experiences: Pre-service teachers' ideas on how they think about and teach science. In *Experiential learning for pre-service science and mathematics teachers: Applications to secondary classrooms*, ed. P. J. Gilmer, L. L. Hahn, and M. R. Spaid, 6–31. Tallahassee FL: Southeast Eisenhower Regional Consortium for Mathematics and Science Education. Also available online at *www. eric.ed.gov*

---

7. Shirley Malcom, personal communication to the authors.

Greenspan, Y. 1999. Scientific inquiry: A journey for a teacher and students. In *Meaningful science: Teachers doing inquiry + teaching science*, ed. T. L. Kielborn and P. J. Gilmer. Tallahassee, FL: Southeast Eisenhower Regional Consortium for Mathematics and Science Education. Also available online at *www.eric.ed.gov*

Hirsch, E., S. Emerick, K. Church, and E. Fuller. 2006. *Teacher working conditions are student learning conditions: A report on the 2006 North Carolina Teacher Working Conditions Survey*. Hillsborough, NC: Center for Teaching Quality.

M. J. Murdock Charitable Trust. 2004. PowerPoint review of the program. Vancouver, WA: M. J. Murdock Charitable Trust.

M. J. Murdock Charitable Trust. n.d. Partners in Science program. *www.murdock-trust.org/ grants/partners-science.php*

Science Teacher and Researcher (STAR) Program. 2008. Evaluating the impact of science teacher as researcher. Report submitted to the Center for Excellence in Science and Mathematics Education at California Polytechnic State University, San Luis Obispo.

Weisbaum, K. S., and D. Huang. 2001. *IISME teacher retention and program impact evaluation 1985–2000*. Cupertino, CA: Industry Initiatives for Science and Math Education. Also available online at *www.iisme.org/PDFfiles/Newsletter.pdf*

Chapter 8

Science Teaching Elsewhere:
Spotlight on Finland

It could be argued that U.S. schooling hasn't gotten any worse in the past 40 years. But the rest of the world has gotten better. For decades the United States had a larger proportion of students in secondary school, by far the largest number and proportion of college goers, and when it came to graduate-level science, the United States set a standard for the entire planet. But that was when Europe was still recovering from the devastations of World War II, Russia was still Soviet, and East and South Asia were only beginning to properly educate their vast populations. Today, we compete with graduates from other countries, and in this chapter we will pose the question, What can we learn from their systems, particularly with regard to science teaching as a profession?

International comparisons of pupils' achievements are straightforward. A sampling of fourth-graders, eighth-graders, and 17-year-olds take a test that is vetted by educators from the participating country. Tests are graded, comparisons made. And, if appropriate, lessons are drawn. But schooling is more difficult to compare because schools are culture-based, their personnel even more so. France and Germany differentiate primary and secondary teachers—even by professional titles (Studienrat [secondary] and Lehrer [primary] in Germany, Professeur [secondary] and Instituteur [or trice] [primary] in France). Teachers in Europe but not in the United States, depending on whether they are primary or secondary, pursue nonoverlapping programs of study at different types of postsecondary institutions. In

Mexico, it is the same where secondary teacher training includes nothing remotely like "the science of teaching" or pedagogy. The United Kingdom and Australia are a bit more like the United States. But in every country, education is competing with the private sector to attract and retain the ablest teachers of science, so some lessons can be drawn.

In this chapter we will focus our main lens on one European country that has made teacher status and satisfaction a top priority, and the result of its efforts.

Finland: A Case Study

In 2000 the world was surprised when "little Finland" bested Singapore, South Korea, the rest of the Asian "tigers," all of Europe, and the United States in the annual international comparison of secondary school math/ science achievement.[1] Not only did Finland's ablest high-school students perform better than their counterparts in other countries, but their lower achievers also bested lower achievers elsewhere, all the while maintaining a high school dropout rate of less than 1%.

The question for educators everywhere was, of course, how? What had Finland been doing to cause Finnish adolescents to achieve such stunning results? Rumor had it the Finns had figured out a way to enhance the professional status of teaching, which, of course, got our attention. In this chapter, we will explore that hypothesis as well as examine other high-achieving nations' responses to the math/science teacher shortage and to the challenge of enhancing student performance.

Higher salaries play a role (see Chapter 5), but only in combination with the "image" (respect awarded) of the profession and tangible opportunities for advancement in their careers. That is the conclusion from a report on the math/science results by the consulting firm McKinsey (McKinsey and Company 2007). Yet higher salaries are available particularly in countries like the Netherlands, where there's a math/science teacher shortage. With a population 1/20th the size of the United States, the Netherlands Ministry of Education set aside nearly $2 billion for salary increases in 2008. Great Britain also dealt with a math/science teacher shortage a decade ago with new money, but instead of earmarking it for teacher salaries, the British started to

---

1. PISA achievement tests are managed by Organization of European Economic Cooperation and Development (OECD). Erkki Aho, an education minister in Finland, is considered the "genius" behind Finland's rise in the achievement competitions.

pay full tuition for college students training to be teachers and an additional stipend for those preparing to teach mathematics and science. This was the policy initiated by Sir Michael Barber, Tony Blair's minister for education from 1995 to 2005. When asked his rationale for Great Britain's policy, Sir Michael answered (in part):

> Great Britain is no Finland but in the past 10–15 years, we changed a bit of everything that had a direct effect on teaching and student achievement. We paid future teachers to train. We gave additional benefits to those preparing to teach mathematics or science…. Teachers are now more respected…by their pupils, and by society as a whole. As a result, the schools are very satisfied with the new cohort of teachers. (Walters 2007)

And by all measures, the new cohort of teachers is satisfied with its work.

Finland, Singapore, and South Korea, in contrast to Great Britain, haven't found it necessary to "buy" future teachers. In Asia, teaching is a valued profession (much like medicine in the United States). There are strict selection procedures for a limited number of teacher education vacancies in the university, and only the best and the brightest applicants are selected for these slots. The reason these countries can manage such a competitive recruiting system is because teaching there has never lost its reputation as a profession of and for high achievers. This is not the case in many countries in Europe or in the United States.

In Finland, teaching jobs are so competitive that there are 10 applicants for every opening (Aho 2008). This, say the experts, is because teaching in Finland, as in Asia, enjoys high status. High status derives from the fact that all teachers must earn a master's degree and complete a major research project before graduating. This sets them apart from other college graduates. Another source of teachers' higher status is that they operate as leaders of teams of specialists, especially when it comes to accommodating lower achieving students.

"No child left behind" in Finland is not achieved with high-stakes testing. Rather, specialized teachers, psychologists, and social workers work with low achievers in class and after school in collaboration with the "master" teacher. Where these team efforts fail, there are "special schools" for such students.

It took the Finns about 30 years to achieve the reforms discussed here, during a period in which there was a Social-Democratic government, a homogeneous population, a Lutheran "work ethic," and a desire to maintain a level playing field. Since 2000, the Finns have had increasing in-migration from multicultural populations, and since 2003 a government having different priorities, says Erkki Aho, Finland's former minister of education; as a result, less of a commitment to equality. Thus, private schools are on the rise, and higher specialized education (in technology, commerce, and marketing) is getting preference over general education. Still, even if Finland's achievement turns out to have been temporary, it is worth detailing one of the several innovations there that have enhanced both teachers' status and their satisfaction.

Finland's Teacher Researcher Net (TRN)

Soon after the Teacher as Researcher movement started in the United Kingdom (in the late 1960s and 1970s), the movement became part of the official development of teacher education in Finland. The term *teacher-researcher* is broadly defined. It ranges from student teachers to retired professors.

By 1994 a formal "Teacher Researcher Net" (TRN) was in place at a major teacher education university (Jyvaskyla), which provides working teachers all over this small country with the means to undertake "action research" in their own classrooms and future (student) teachers to do supervised field research. Student teachers freely choose the topic of their theses and complete their practice in the school of a teacher who is a member of the TRN, by turning entire schools into "field research schools." Contrast this with the kind of research academics are funded to do in the United States, employing complicated research methodologies and engaging mainly doctoral candidates. The study model chosen by the Finns "offers student (teachers) experience in collegial work, ongoing inquiry of teaching and shared curriculum building. As a result the student teachers have more time to reflect on their own professional growth" (Jakku-Sihvonen and Niemi 2006, pp. 103ff).

Here's a list of some of the goals of the TRN in Finland. Compare these with the 12 elements of professionalism listed in Chapter 3:

- Provide opportunities for student teachers to work in different environment.

- Offer teacher-researchers, student teachers, and teacher educators an open forum for discussion.

- Enhance appreciation of teachers' work in our society.

- Improve teachers' opportunities to develop their own work.

- Develop teacher-researchers to become a significant part of the educational paradigm in Finland.

- Offer teacher-researchers opportunities for postgraduate studies at the university.

The point is that the Finns have found a way to bridge theory and practice and to include not only professors of education but also working teachers in scholarly forums.

In the beginning, Finland's TRN operated through working conferences (1994–1998); later (1999) through summer schools. Topics range from teaching techniques (e.g., the "Hungarian method" of teaching mathematics) to what would be considered "policy issues" here. Funding was available to bring in foreign specialists and to send working teachers abroad to continue their inquiries.

Thus has Finland bridged the gulf between the college faculty and the working teacher. The result has been research studies that have more immediacy and relevance to the classroom teacher and higher self-esteem for teachers/researchers as a cohort.

Benefits to Science Teachers

While the TRN in Finland serves teachers at all levels and in all subject areas, from the outset particular attention has been given to the teaching of science. The very first special issue of the *Journal of Teacher as Researcher* focused on "Chemistry Using Natural Substances." Since then there have been others focusing on the teaching of chemistry, mathematics, and physics. The journal itself directly contributes to teachers' increased self-esteem by providing a shared channel of publication for teacher-researchers, student teachers, and teacher educators, which is rare in other countries.

Because Finland is part of Europe, its teachers are also supported for travel to international conferences and encouraged to collaborate with teachers/researchers from other countries. Note that travel, international collaboration, research support, and publication are perks and satisfactions reserved in the United States to the college faculty. Access to these perks contributes to Finnish teachers' higher status in the community and to their overall higher self-esteem. Reflecting on 10 years of TRN activities, the Finnish Educational Research Association sees "teacher empowerment" as essential to enhanced professional status:

For an individual teacher, the [TRN has been] a source of empowerment through which his/her professionalism grows and in which s/he can share in it. ...The Net has built a bridge between the institution of teacher education and the teachers working in the field schools. The seminars, summer schools, and workshops have provided a platform to meet and discuss current education phenomena and to support the teachers' career and academic educational goals. (Jakku-Sihvonen and Niemi 2006, p. 117).

All very well—for Finland. What would it take to conceptualize and fund a version of the TRN in the United States?

References

Aho, E. 2008. Interview. *NRC Handelsblad* (April 19). Trans. Sheila Tobias.

Jakku-Sihvonen, R., and H. Niemi, eds. 2006. *Research-based teacher education in Finland: Reflections by Finnish teacher-educators*. Helsinki, Finland: Finnish Educational Research Association.

McKinsey and Company. 2007. *How the world's best-performing school systems come out on top*. Washington, DC: McKinsey and Company. Also available online at *www.mckinsey. com/App_Media/Reports/SSO/Worlds_School_Systems_Final.pdf*

Walters, D. 2007. Hoger salaris voor leraren lost probleem niet op in Nederland. *NRC Handelsblad* (November 12). Trans. Sheila Tobias.

Chapter 9

Empowering Science Teachers to Lead

The levers of power, switches that are turned on and off to make a school system run, are seldom in the hands of teachers.

(Macroff 1988, p. 76)

For too long, teachers have allowed others to make work-related decisions for them. Science teachers need to see themselves as the key to the success of the educational enterprise. To that end, they must help legislators, governors, and school boards understand what schools need to meet the nation's educational goals.

For teachers to be heard, they must take the first steps. They need to

- get their views on our educational system published by writing op-ed pieces, letters to the editor, and letters to public officials;

- speak out at school board meetings;

- take on advocacy roles such as forming internet communities and other action groups to address school improvement;

- participate in educational reform groups;

- ferret out young emergent teachers with leadership gifts and encourage them to take on leadership roles in the school and the educational community; and

- sing the praises of outstanding science teachers, especially those who are too humble to do so themselves.

All of this is particularly urgent in the coming five years because the many science disciplines may join math and reading in high-stakes accountability systems.

Who will represent the secondary science teacher in the debates that are sure to follow about the nature and uses of the science test? One thing we have learned in talking with and hearing from hundreds of secondary science teachers is, as we've been arguing in this book, secondary science teachers are a unique breed. They inhabit three distinct groups. They are teachers, and like all teachers, constrained by state and district laws and rulings. They are science specialists with different and additional responsibilities for lab-based teaching that other secondary teachers do not have. And, when they are given the opportunity to participate in professional scientists' labs and symposia, they are members of the wider world of science.

One additional and important observation we have made is that fewer secondary science teachers are represented in formal educational governance than teachers from other subject specialties. Either we find ways to tempt them into positions like these, or we invent alternate structures to give them voice outside and over their classroom and their school.

Recommendation One: Attracting Science Teachers to School and District Governance

We began, several chapters ago, with a science-teacher-produced power matrix (see page 21), indicating who among the various players in the school and in the school district make critical decisions that affect science teachers' professional work. That power matrix revealed that—at least for our respondents—decisions as to curriculum, pacing, teaching assignments, and lab materials are made by others. Certain new structures, such as professional learning communities (see Chapter 6), could balance the top-down decision tree with teacher-generated recommendations—but only, as we have seen, if the principal and the district administrators are willing to share power. Then, there are individual states' mandates and federal interest in teaching and learning—farther still removed from the arena in which science teachers operate and have any input at all.

These observations led us to inquire, How well represented is the special nature of science teaching among those who make the rules? More specifically, are school administrators whose original teaching certification is in science proportionately represented among school principals? District administrators? State school officers? Federal policy makers? The answer, it appears, is "not at all." But even more interesting is how underexamined this question is.

There are approximately 14,000 school districts in the United States, each with a district superintendent, the larger ones having numerous assistant superintendents and financial and other specialists in addition. Most (except for the financial specialists) will have been teachers at some point in their lives. But rarely is the subject matter of that individual's earlier teaching recorded.

The California listings identify superintendents by their gender and ethnicity but not subject matter of origin. A mid-decade study of *The State of the American School Superintendency* by the American Association of School Administrators, the parent organization of school superintendents, doesn't even ask the question on its 60-item questionnaire (Glass and Granceschini 2007). (Prodded by the authors, the organization has agreed to ask this question on its next and subsequent surveys.) We were unable to query state by state, but where we had contacts (as in Arizona and Connecticut) we found (in Connecticut) that only 6 out of 189 district superintendents had ever taught science.[1]

Even more significant are some deeply held prejudices among the non–science educated superintendents we have interviewed. We do not have a significant sample, but their explanation for the lack of science teacher administrators are remarkably similar. "Science teachers don't really want to be administrators. They prefer the isolation (Isolation? In a classroom of 30 students?) of their classrooms and labs." "They don't handle people well." "They don't want to interact with the community." Or, from the one science-teacher-turned-administrator we had the privilege of interviewing, "Science teachers don't like to operate in the political world of administration." To triangulate our findings, limited as they were, we inquired of a major national superintendent education doctorate program where, among the candidates for the degree, only a handful were certified in science.

We did find (through one of our website inquiries) a few dozen science teachers who aspire to be superintendents.[2] Their perceptions of the job and their reasons for applying indicate that they, too, are concerned with the lack of representation of science teachers in educational leadership. Part of the reason they have chosen eventually to leave their classrooms and move into administration is, they tell us, that science education is not receiving the attention it

---

1. Suzanne Taylor, Adjunct Professor, Schmidt Labor Research Center, University of Rhode Island, personal communication to the authors.

2. A copy of the interview protocol we used with our superintendent aspirants can be found on page 146.

deserves, and that too often directives about how science should be taught are coming from people with little or no science teaching expertise.

An AP chemistry teacher from California who just completed her administrative credential in hopes of becoming a principal next year and eventually a superintendent says, "Everyone [in education] knows that science is important, but because they are not well-versed in the subject, many of the people I have studied with do not know in what direction to take science education."

When asked why science teachers are so underrepresented in high-ranking administrative positions, our aspiring superintendents, remarkably, use the same language as the superintendents we interviewed: Most science teachers do not want to "put up with the politics" of administration. "Science teachers are more analytical in thought, less diplomatic, and do not do well in the bureaucracy," explains one of our aspirants. But others point to lack of encouragement to move into leadership because good science teachers are so hard to replace.

All of our respondents said, in one way or another, that most science teachers they know love what they are doing and feel they have more impact in the classroom. But the aspirants we interviewed believe they would have much to contribute if they were to come to the decision-making tables.

For one, they are experienced problem solvers; they see themselves as being quick to recognize and analyze problems, finding a variety of solutions and measuring the effects of any proposed change. For another, they recognize the importance of a solid science curriculum in preparing students for the jobs of the future and are committed to that goal. They know from their own personal experience that science has to be more than something students learn. It has to be something students enjoy doing!

Even if our dozen or so interviewees achieve superintendent positions of their own, moving a few more science teachers into formal positions of power won't re-balance the skew. But what about empowering some of the organizations in which science teachers do find themselves?

To explore some alternate strategies, we have met with local science chairs, representatives from the National Science Teachers Association, members of the Association of Science Teacher Educators, and the National Science Education Leadership Association, a small but potentially potent association of science teacher leaders. From these conversations has emerged another strategy for empowerment outlined in the next section.

Recommendation Two: Establish Science Teacher Councils

This project, as we have said more than once, originated in the authors' meeting with a group of 10 local science chairs from as many high schools in Pima County, Arizona. The chairs—who on average hired, fired, and supervised 10 science teachers each—provided us and one another during those long dinner meetings, sponsored by Research Corporation for Science Advancement, with a detailed analysis of the needs of students and teachers in their schools. We were struck then and now—when they told us they were meeting for the first time—that our science chairs had never before been called on as a group to provide any kind of leadership in their school districts. In short, no outside body had shown any interest prior to ours in mining their considerable combined expertise, or using them in other ways to represent secondary science.

This makes us imagine an alternative to the standard route to administration, one that empowers "science teacher councils" made up of science chairs from an entire district (or county) merged with some equivalent group from elementary and middle school. The science teacher council would be charged with participating in a range of activities now entirely the purview of principals and district administrators, including, but not limited to the following.

- *Hiring.* The district's science teacher council would first establish criteria for hiring decisions, then develop the search process, and later participate in selections. Postsecondary science teachers from a local community or four-year college could be included, though the science council made up of secondary chairs would minimally co-preside, depending on the level of hire. The principal or superintendent could have veto power. But the entire process would be collaborative, with the science council providing input and expertise.

- *Teacher assessment, promotion, retention, and evaluation.* Science teachers would be evaluated on a range of criteria, including but not solely limited to student test scores, with peer evaluation a guaranteed part of employment policy. The principal or superintendent could veto a decision, but the science teacher council would preside over the process.

- *Decisions about standards, curriculum, and student assessments.* State departments of education and national organizations provide science standards and may well recommend various tests. But each district's science teacher council would decide whether to use existing standards, curriculum, and assessments. If a school district wants to require more rigorous science than the state, it can. But in our scenario, the science teacher council would have to make a scientifically defensible decision and include ways to measure success.

Why wouldn't those who administer a revised No Child Left Behind, or whatever federal mandate replaces the act, *not* want each core subject area to have its own teacher council for each district (with smaller districts combined)? After all, teachers—by NCLB's own measures—are the single most important variable in instruction.

In time, we would predict, the local science teacher councils will constitute a natural affinity group and, with support from some of the national associations (NSTA, ASTE, perhaps even the science societies) be called on to meet regionally and/or nationally even to testify.

Recommendation Three: New Alliances Within the Science Community

In our survey of science education reforms over the past 20 years, we uncovered two that we believe have real potential for increasing the power of science teachers to alter the parameters that restrict their professional lives. One is the Kenan Fellows program in North Carolina, which trains teacher leaders to lobby state legislative bodies, organize themselves and fellow teachers around school and state-based issues, and overall take power back from those who do not have a science teaching background.

The other is the array of summer research opportunities available to secondary science teachers that brings them into contact with working scientists and engineers in some of the national labs, with university researchers, and in private business. These projects are so far modest, but with wider adoption by the Department of Energy, additional funding from foundations and others, such summer work could eventually affect thousands instead of hundreds of secondary science teachers, affording them not only an upgrading of their skills and knowledge base, but also an extension of their networks and an expanded power base.

At that point we would hope that teachers from a single school be sent as a cohort to these programs as a way of strengthening their power to make change. Scientists and otherwise active science professionals tend to carry more political weight in a community than science teachers. Once the scientist gets to know well the secondary science program in one local school, another kind of partnership may ensue, one that the school district administrator didn't count on.

What the United States needs are ongoing collaborations between science teachers and scientists. Ideally they will meet in summer research programs—the kind described in Chapter 7. But however they manage to make contact, science teachers must find ways to join forces with scientists as activists in the communities where they both reside. This way science educators can capitalize on scientists' greater political prowess to promote and strengthen the critical role of science teachers in their work.

The Next New Student Population

If science teachers are to lead, they must pay attention to where students, technology, jobs, and the nation's priorities are headed.

For example, look at the students sitting in our classrooms today. They are the Web 2.0 generation, used to mounting their own websites, researching on Google, uploading their videos, and text messaging their thoughts. As such, they are challenging teachers at least as profoundly as any who came before them. Science teachers seem naturally positioned to take the first steps in creating the new curriculum and to lobby for the equipment that meets the needs of this tech-savvy population.

Science and technology are inseparable in the 21st century. Science teachers know they need the resources to connect their students in real-time to the world of science: to experiments like those of the International Space Station—NASA, NOAA, etc.—to databases, and to working scientists wherever they might be. And this means that science classrooms must have the technology that allows students to interact with science and scientists via the internet.

But, as a wide-ranging review of technology and education in a recent edition of *Science* makes us aware, "…technology is not a magic bullet for education. A fancy bit of electronics distributed without context and support may leave the laptop functioning as a doorstop" (Hines, Jasny, and Mervis 2009, p. 53).

Whether a new technology will be a magic bullet or a doorstop will depend on who makes the critical decisions about what to install. Any new technology needs to be selected by science teachers, operating not just as end-users, but as members of a strategic technology team that will investigate, select, finance, and, once installed, train their counterparts to integrate the new technology into their teaching.

Thus, if they are to serve their students in a Web 2.0 environment, science teachers will need to be where decisions are made. Only they can persuade their schools, school boards, local businesses, and the wider community for the full integration of technology into their classrooms. Whether this effort originates with science chairs, local NSTA memberships, the local science community, or other entities in this, as in so many different aspects of their work, it is to everyone's advantage that science teachers take the lead.

References

Glass, T. E., and L. A. Granceschini. 2007. *The state of the American school superintendency: A mid-decade study.* Published in partnership with the American Association of School Administrators. Lanham, MD: Rowman & Littlefield.

Hines, P. J., B. R. Jasny, and J. Mervis. 2009. Adding a T to the three R's. *Science* (January 2): 53.

Maeroff, G. I. 1988. *The empowerment of teachers: Overcoming the crisis of confidence.* New York: Teachers College Press.

About the Authors

Sheila Tobias has made a science and an art of being a curriculum outsider. Neither a mathematician nor a scientist, she has tackled the question of why intelligent and motivated college students have specific difficulties in certain disciplines, particularly mathematics and science. From her work have come seven books on math/science teaching and learning, three commissioned by Research Corporation for Science Advancement: *Overcoming Math Anxiety* (W. W. Norton, 1995), *Succeed with Math: Every Student's Guide to Conquering Math Anxiety* (College Board, 1987), and *They're Not Dumb, They're Different: Stalking the Second Tier* (RCSA, 1990); *Breaking the Science Barrier: How to Explore and Understand the Sciences* (with physicist Carl Tomizuka; College Board, 1992); *Revitalizing Undergraduate Science: Why Some Things Work and Most Don't* (RCSA, 1992); *The Hidden Curriculum: Faculty-Made Tests in College Science* (with Jacqueline Raphael; Springer, 1997); and *Rethinking Science as a Career* (RCSA, 1995).

For *Science Teaching as a Profession: Why It Isn't. How It Could Be*, Tobias has teamed with Anne Baffert to chart the challenges faced by secondary science teachers today. Baffert has been teaching high school science for 15 years in public and private schools in California and Arizona. She has taught all levels of biology, chemistry, physical science, and astrobiology and is currently the chair of the science department and teacher of chemistry at Salpointe Catholic High School in Tucson, Arizona.

Glossary of Education Terms

AFT	American Federation of Teachers
ASTE	Association for Science Teacher Education
AYP	Annual Yearly Progress
DOE	Department of Energy
IISME	Industry Initiatives for Science and Mathematics Education
NBC	National Board Certification
NBCT	National Board Certified Teacher
NCLB	No Child Left Behind Act
NEA	National Education Association
NSTA	National Science Teachers Association
PiS	Partners in Science program
PLC	Professional Learning Community
RCSA	Research Corporation for Science Advancement
STAR	Science Teacher and Researcher program
STEM	Science, Technology, Engineering, and Mathematics

Recommended Resources

T. M. Stinnet, *Professional Problems of Teachers* (Macmillan, 1968), and the author's edited collection of essays titled *The Teacher Dropout* (Phi Delta Kappan, 1970).

Richard Ingersoll's *Who Controls Teachers' Work? Power and Accountability in America's Schools* (Harvard University Press, 2006) is useful because the author, uniquely in our review of the literature, focuses not only on teachers' need for status, privilege, and autonomy, but also on "power" as well as accountability. He identifies decision making and control as essential elements of professional life that we found in our interviews and in our respondents' statements to be relevant, too.

Ivor F. Goodson's edited volume *Studying Teachers' Lives* (Teachers College Press, 1992) provides both substantive and methodological support for studies of teachers' lives. Because that's what we are trying to do in this book, we appreciated the scholarly support.

A Nation at Risk: The Imperative for Education Reform (National Commission on Excellence in Education, 1983).

Judith Warren Little and Milbrey Wallin McLaughlin's *Teacher's Work: Individuals, Colleagues, and Contexts* (Teachers College Press, 1993) includes a set of individual case studies (such as a study of a performing arts high school) and a provocative alternate model of Michael Huberman's called "Teacher as Artisan."

The definitive defense of teachers and teaching *What Matters Most: Teaching for America's Future*, issued by the National Commission on Teaching and America's Future, 1996.

Though having to do with arts and humanities teachers, we found in Gene I. Maeroff's *The Empowerment of Teachers: Overcoming the Crisis of Confidence* (Teachers College Press, 1988) a remarkable precursor to our own observations and analysis. The book covers topics such as salary issues, misunderstandings between administrators and teachers, institutionalizing change, collaborations between teachers and college scholars, and unions, and provides an entire chapter on teachers' access to power.

For an overview of the many means of providing teacher accountability, apart from students' test scores, we consulted Kenneth D. Peterson's *Teacher Evaluation: A Comprehensive Guide to New Directions and Practices* (Corwin Press, 2000).

As background for science teaching in the current era, we consulted The National Research Council's *National Science Education Standards* (National Academy Press, 1996).

And then there was Amitai Etzioni's edited volume, *The Semi-Professions and Their Organization: Teachers, Nurses, Social Workers* (Macmillan, 1969), which lumps teaching, nursing, and social work together as presumptuous in claiming to be "professions" when they are at best semi-professions.

Recent books and reports focused on one or more of our topics include the following:

For an analysis of the causes and cures of the STEM teacher shortfall, see the Committee on Prospering in the Global Economy of the 21st Century, *Rising Above the Gathering Storm: Energizing and Employing America for a Brighter Economic Future* (National Academies Press, 2005).

And for another view from the National Science Board, *A National Action Plan for Addressing the Critical Needs of the U.S. Science Technology, Engineering and Mathematics Education System* (National Science Foundation, 2007).

On teachers' pay, Daniel Moulthrop, Ninive Clements Calegari, and Dave Eggers, with a provocative title, *Teachers Have It Easy: The Big Sacrifices and Small Salaries of America's Teachers* (W. W. Norton, 2006).

Though we do not cover charter schools, there being too little information about teachers of secondary science (and secondary charter schools in general), we did find Robert Maranto, Scott Milliman, Frederick Hess, and April Gresham's *School Choice in the Real World: Lessons From Arizona Charter Schools* (Westview, 1999) to be useful.

Also, on the KIPP Schools, Jay Mathews's *Work Hard. Be Nice.: How Two Inspired Teachers Created the Most Promising Schools in America* (Algonquin Books, 2009).

On professional learning communities, Louise Stoll and Karen Seashore Louis's *Professional Learning Communities: Divergence, Depth and Dilemmas* (Open University Press, 2007).

On No Child Left Behind and high-stakes testing, Sharon L. Nichols and David C. Berliner's, *Collateral Damage: How High-Stakes Testing Corrupts America's Schools* (Harvard Education Press, 2007), and Berliner's earlier book, with Bruce J. Biddle, *The Manufactured Crisis: Myths, Fraud, and the Attack on America's Public Schools* (Basic Books, 1995).

Richard Rothstein, ed., *Grading Education: Getting Accountability Right* (Teachers College Press, 2008) and Richard D. Kahlenberg, ed., *Improving on No Child Left Behind: Getting Education Reform Back on Track* (Century Foundation Press, 2008).

On what makes science teaching and learning different from other subjects, we liked Sarah Michaels, Andrew W. Shouse, and Heidi A. Schweingruber's *Ready, Set, Science! Putting Research to Work in K–8 Science Classrooms* (National Academies Press, 2008).

For a discussion of the backgrounds and special challenges of school superintendents, Thomas E. Glass and Louis A. Franceschini's *The State of the American School Superintendency: A Mid-Decade Study* (Rowman & Littefield, 2007).

From the hundreds of scholarly and popular articles about science education, high-stakes testing, and teachers' status, we found especially useful articles by Linda Darling-Hammond, in particular, "Teacher Quality and Student Achievement: A Review of State Policy Evidence" (2000), *Education Policy Analysis Archives* 8 (1), and R. M. Ingersoll, "Teacher Turnover and Teacher Shortages: An Organizational Analysis" (2001), *American Educational Research Journal*, 38 (3): 499–534.

For what we consider to be the threat to the sanctity of teacher certification, teacher tenure, and teacher autonomy, Robert Gordon, Thomas J. Kane, and Douglas O. Staiger's various writings, especially their book *The Hamilton Project: Identifying Effective Teachers Using Performance on the Job* (Brookings Institution, 2006).

And for an overview of the presidential administration's education plans, President Barack Obama and Vice President Joe Biden's *Plan for Lifetime Success Through Education*, issued in January 2009 (see *www.barackobama.com/pdf/issues/PreK-12EducationFactSheet.pdf*).

Interview Protocols

Standard Teacher Interview

Date	
Teacher's name/school	
School demographics	
E-mail address	
Years in teaching profession	
Subjects (levels) taught	
Hours spent at school/week	
Total hours spent/week (grading, prep, and teaching)	
Number of preps	
Major/minor in college	

1. If you are NOT teaching in your major field, explain how have you have compensated/educated yourself to teach your subject? As well as kept up with the changes in your field?

2. Do you expect to be teaching five years from now? Ten years from now? Why or why not?

3. Do you feel that the demands of teaching science are more or less challenging than teaching other subjects?

4. Are there reasons it might be harder to keep secondary science teachers in the profession, as opposed to teachers in other subjects?

5. What are the most satisfying aspects of your secondary science teaching career/job?

6. What do you need to stay/be more satisfied in this career?

7. How much input do you feel you have on:

   - Your working conditions
   - The curriculum
   - Your teaching assignments
   - Hiring decisions within your school/department

8. What kind of staff support do you have?

9. Could you use more help preparing labs and doing paperwork?

10. Aside from an increase in salary, what could be done to improve your work life? What would you consider to be the least satisfying aspect of your job?

11. If you have a concern about your working conditions or your treatment as a professional, who do you go to? Do you feel that your needs are addressed? Who listens?

12. Do you feel that anything is being done to help improve your working conditions, and if so by whom?

13. What would make your teaching more effective?

14. How did you know that you are a good teacher? Have you been recognized or acknowledged in any way?

Questions for New Teachers

Major in college

Subject(s) taught

Type of school

State

1. How long have you been teaching?

2. Do you expect to be teaching in five years? In 10 years? Why or why not?

3. How does your firsthand experience with teaching differ from what you had first anticipated?

4. What has been your greatest surprise in teaching?

5. What has been your greatest disappointment?

6. Aside from an increase in salary, what could be done to improve your work life? What would you consider to be the least satisfying aspect of your job?

Questions for Teachers Who Have Left the Profession

Date

Teacher's name/school

School demographics

E-mail address

1. How many years were you in the teaching profession? In what type of school?
2. What subject(s) were you teaching?
3. What was the reason you gave for leaving the profession?
4. Why did you REALLY leave the profession?
5. What could be done to bring you back to the profession?
6. What could have happened to prevent you from leaving the profession in the first place?
7. How does pay/benefits/tenure compare (current job and teaching)?

Questions for Principals

Date

Principal's name/school

School demographics

E-mail address

Years in administration

Subjects (levels) taught as teacher

1. Do you feel that the demands of teaching science are more or less challenging than teaching other subjects?
2. Are there reasons it might be harder to keep secondary science teachers in the profession, as opposed to teachers in other subjects?
3. Why do you think secondary math/science teachers leave teaching?
4. What do you believe could stave off the attrition of teachers (science/math in particular)?
5. What are you as a principal able to do to hold onto and attract good teachers?

Aspiring Superintendent Interview

Name

Date

Subject(s) taught

Years teaching science

Type of school

1. Why are you leaning toward becoming a school superintendent?

2. Was there an issue, an event, or a person that impelled you in this direction?

3. How will your science teaching background contribute to the decisions you will make about science curriculum and instruction as a superintendent?

4. As a superintendent, what do you believe you could do to stave the attrition of teachers (science/math in particular)?

5. Why do so few science teachers take the administrative route to powerful positions in the district?

6. What would make such positions more appealing/attractive to them? How do we attract more science teachers to the superintendency?

7. What do you anticipate when the "science test" is introduced in 2009? How it will change science teaching and science teachers' lives?

Index